Spiritual Experiences in Life and Therapy

William Blake Paul, MA, LMFT

© 2020

Introduction

I am a member of the Church of Jesus Christ of Latter-day Saints. I am a Licensed Marriage and Family Therapist (LMFT). This book is a result of my personal experiences with spirituality, my understanding of the doctrines of the Church, and my professional experiences as an LMFT. It should be of interest to members of the Church, members of traditional Christian churches, and all mental health professionals who believe in phenomena beyond human or mechanical senses.

This book begins with my personal spiritual experiences. It adds teachings of the Church. Then it compares and contrasts these with scientific research. Then it adds spiritual experiences of my clients.

Most of the therapeutic experiences in this book come from my clients in California. Some are members of the Church of Jesus Christ of Latter-day Saints. Most are not. I usually don't differentiate who is who because it's not important to the spiritual nature of the experiences themselves.

This book interprets spiritual experiences according to doctrines unique to the Church of Jesus Christ of Latter-day Saints. Some have similarities to doctrines of traditional Christianity; some do not.

What makes a study unique to the Church of Jesus Christ of Latter-day Saints? It is not just that the subjects of the study are members of the Church because the researchers may not be members. It is not just that the researchers are members of the Church because they may perform research that any researcher could do. It is that the unique doctrines found in the Church are used in the study. In other words, the study investigates doctrines that are unique to the Church, and/or the study interprets results and draws conclusions based on doctrines unique to the Church.

In this understanding, many studies of and by members of the Church of Jesus Christ of Latter-day Saints, although important in general scientific investigation, are neutral as to the unique doctrines of the Church. For example, a study of attitudes of BYU students towards rape could be conducted by members of Church and could be about members, but if it does not involve doctrines that are unique to the Church, it is analogous to any study done by anyone about anyone.

I feel like I could continue writing and revising forever. I have purposely left out some of my most sacred experiences. I have also left out my beliefs about some controversial topics. At some point, I just have to stop revising and publish this book as it is.

My Testimony of Heavenly Father and Jesus Christ

When I was thirteen years old, I went to camp with the Boy Scouts of America. Saturday evening, we had a Church meeting. A recently returned missionary talked passionately about the Holy Spirit. I don't know his name or what he said, but he awoke in me a desire to find out for myself if God lived.

After the meeting, I went to sleep in my tent. The next morning, I woke up in a puddle of water. The Scouts were teasing each other and making inappropriate jokes. It was a stark contrast to the Holy Spirit I felt the night before.

I walked to the place where the return missionary had talked, and to the very spot he had stood. I saw a path trailing off into the woods. I followed it.

I can't describe what happened next. The woods appeared to be vibrant with life, color, and sound. It seemed that all my senses were heightened. My heart was overpowered with awe and gratitude for Heavenly Father's creations. I knelt on the ground to pray. The Holy Spirit confirmed to my soul that Heavenly Father lived. I opened my eyes, and I seemed to see proof of God's existence in every particle of His creation. This testimony has stayed with me to this day.

Shortly afterwards, I was praying at night, and I was convicted of my sins. I knew I had chosen to do wrong. I felt remorse. I knew there was nothing I could do to fix myself. I prayed for forgiveness. I felt my guilt and shame taken away. I was amazed and began to cry. I prayed, "Lord, how is it done?" (Enos 1:7).

Enos 1:8 came into my mind, "Because of thy faith in Christ, whom thou hast never before heard nor seen." I knew that Jesus Christ had paid the penalty for my sins and was my Savior.

<u>Personal Relationship</u>

Jesus Christ knows me by name. He knows my strengths and weaknesses, my obedience, my faults and foibles, and all of my sins. He has suffered for my sins. He is involved in the details of my life. I know it through experience.

Soon after I gained a testimony of Heavenly Father and Jesus Christ, I was sitting in Sunday School, watching a video about the Seattle Temple, then under construction. The Holy Spirit told me that I would go into that Temple someday. This was totally unexpected and left me feeling baffled. I liked the video, but as a young teenager, I had no plans to go to Seattle! Of course, that came true in my life. Why did the Lord tell me that? I imagine it was His way of letting me know that He is omnipotent. I believe He knows everything I will do in my life. This knowledge doesn't bother me or make me feel like I don't have freedom of choice. I do. A Scientist knows that a rat in a maze will eventually find the cheese. The father of the Prodigal Son knew he would come back. The Lord knows I'd make mistakes and eventually come around!

At the end of my mission, my Mission President,

who managed us missionaries, gave me specific warnings about problems that would arise in my life. I thought, "I bet he says that to all the missionaries." I didn't heed those warnings, and I had problems in all of those specific areas! This was a further testimony to me that the Lord knew what I would go through.

My Mission President told me to not be in a hurry to get married, but when I met the right person, don't wait to be married. I was in a hurry to be married despite what he said.

I went to Brigham Young University. At the beginning of one religion class, I had been thinking about a quote attributed to Brigham Young that unmarried men over twenty-five years old are a menace to society. My teacher said he felt inspired that morning to talk to us about that specific quote. He cautioned us about feeling bad about that quote as it could take some of us longer to find our eternal companions. He said he was twenty-seven when he got married. I thought, "Surely, he can't be saying that because of me!" After it took me a long time to find the right woman to marry, I believe that he said that just for my sake.

One Sunday, my car was broken down, and I was walking to Church. A pickup truck pulled over. It was a brother from the Ward. He said the Spirit told him, "Give my son a ride." I didn't even need a ride; I was a few blocks from the Church. As I thought about the experience, I was grateful and humbled that God called me his son and cared enough to tell someone else that!

Sacred Experiences

We are commanded to bear testimony of spiritual experiences. In Acts 22:15, Ananias tells Paul, "For thou shalt be his witness unto all men of what thou hast seen and heard." Jesus commanded his apostles to "go ye into all the world, and preach the gospel to every creature" (Mark 16:15).

Spiritual experiences should not be shared with everyone. In verse 18, Paul is commanded to leave Jerusalem because the people will not receive his testimony. In other words, Paul was told not to share his experience with the people because they would not receive it. Furthermore, Matthew 7:6 says, "Give not that which is holy unto the dogs, neither cast ye your pearls before swine, lest they trample them under their feet, and turn again and rend you." We must take our audience into account before we share spiritual experiences.

Some spiritual experiences are too sacred to be shared with anyone. In 2 Corinthians 12:4, Paul says, "He was caught up into paradise, and heard unspeakable words, which it is not lawful for a man to utter." As I was writing this book, I heard that if you share sacred things that aren't meant to be shared, God may not bless you with more.

How do we know which spiritual experiences to share and which are too sacred? In my own life, I have had to rely on divine inspiration to know what to share and when to share it. I have written my most sacred experiences in a journal, and I share them with fellow believers, but a published book is not the appropriate place for them.

Avoiding Talking about the Devil

The Church of Jesus Christ of Latter-day Saints teaches extensively about the pre-existence, including about how Lucifer and his followers fell from Heaven. Lucifer became Satan, the devil. The Church teaches that the devil and his followers tempt us here on earth. However, leaders of the Church do not encourage going into great detail about the devil. Elder Jeffrey R. Holland, an Apostle, said, "We don't talk about the adversary any more than we have to, and I don't like talking about him at all" ("We Are All Enlisted," General Conference, October 2011).

In my own experience, I have received similar cautionary guidance from the Holy Spirit. One of my clients said she was a witch. She told me lots of details about her practices. I approached her case like any other, listening from a detached and objective scientific view, and taking notes. After she left, I began typing the notes as usual. The Holy Spirit distinctly impressed upon me not to type notes about her practices, that I should not share what I had learned, good as my intentions may be.

Soon afterwards, I was at home, looking for something online when I came across a testimony by a Christian who had practiced witchcraft before converting.

I didn't think there was anything wrong with reading it because it was written by a Christian. I began reading about the Christian's former life, but was immediately cautioned not to read any further. I stopped reading and closed the page.

Saying anything about the devil is like treading on thin ice. Therefore, I will do my best to follow the Holy Spirit and relate only what is necessary to my experiences in therapy.

God Has Complete Power over the Devil

Heavenly Father could control us but doesn't want to do so. The devil wants to control us but can't because God won't allow him to do so. He is like a spring ever pushing upward and Heavenly Father is like a strong arm pushing down on that spring. Because Heavenly Father is stronger than the spring, He has complete control over the spring, allowing it to rise or pushing it down at His discretion.

In the First Vision, we see that the devil had the power to destroy Joseph Smith and would have done so; however, this would have gone against the spiritual laws of existence, namely moral agency, so Heavenly Father did not allow it.

The devil *does* have power over us, when we give into temptation. That is why we are told to "speedily repent" (Doctrine and Covenants 109:21). Imagine that you are walking with your much older and wiser brother and an angry bully threatens to beat you up. You notice that the bully fears your brother. You become cocky and make faces at the bully. The bully becomes even angrier and says, "Someday your brother won't be here to protect you!"

Your brother warns you to stay out of the bully's territory. One day when your brother is not around, you carelessly wander into the bully's territory. The bully finds you alone. He is elated and exclaims, "Your brother can't save you now!" He begins beating you mercilessly. You call your older brother, who comes running, and the bully runs away. Your brother picks you up, carries you home, and nurses your wounds. The lesson is that Jesus Christ will protect us from the devil as long as we don't give into temptation. The more we give into temptation, the more power the devil will have power over us, even to our own destruction.

The devil cannot pick up a gun and shoot anyone. This would be against moral law. The devil can, however, tempt humans to do so and does successfully as any glance at the news will confirm. The devil doesn't *force* them to shoot someone, but tempts them to become so angry that they *choose* to do so.

The Devil's Influence

On my mission, I became more aware of the devil's influence. In the middle of a spiritual discussion with investigators, children would fight, pets would misbehave, pornography would come on the television, or any number of other things would happen to hinder the Holy

Spirit and the conversion process. When investigators tried to come to Church, cars would break down or other emergencies would arise. Many returned missionaries could tell similar stories.

Missionaries also told me that devil worship was really big in Utah. I was surprised and asked how that could be. They quoted Joseph Smith that "in relation to the kingdom of God, the devil always sets up his kingdom at the very same time in opposition to God (History of the Church 6:354).

On my mission, I was sheltered from the evil influences on television and in music. When I returned home, I was shocked at how much worse things had become in two years. Since then, I've watched the world progress from wickedness to deeper wickedness. What young people today view as normal, I view as rapid spiritual decline in my short lifetime! I realize that I would have been shocked at the television and music from my youth if I hadn't been conditioned to accept it as normal.

Even more importantly, I began seeing the corruption of government. Paul, the Apostle, spoke about this when he said, "For we wrestle not against flesh and blood, but against principalities, against powers, against the rulers of the darkness of this world, against spiritual wickedness in high places" (Ephesians 6:12).

The devil is amassing power in any area possible—religious, governmental, military, cultural, economic, and spiritual to name a few.

Temptation

An elaborate temptation happened to a friend of mine in California. He set a date to go to the Temple for the first time and be baptized for his father and other relatives. He unexpectedly got a call from an old colleague to be her assistant on the Sports Illustrated swimsuit shoot photo shoot. The swimsuits were to be painted on the models. Additionally, my friend would be paid a lot of money that he desperately needed. He and I marveled at the timing of the offer. It was the same day we were going to the Temple! Of course, my friend and I went to the temple, and he was baptized for his father and other relatives. It was a wonderful experience!

Science and Spirituality

The finest trick of the devil is to persuade you that he does not exist—Charles Baudelaire

Materialists say that nothing is real that cannot be observed with the five senses. Paradoxically, they accept that much, if not most, of the matter in the Universe is "dark matter," invisible matter that has similar properties to visible matter, like gravitational pull. That sounds a lot like something "spiritual"!

Spirit Matter

Traditional Christianity believes in spirit, but says that it is altogether different than matter. Materialists say that nothing exists that is not matter. Both have a part of the truth. Joseph Smith taught, "There is no such thing as immaterial matter. All spirit is matter, but it is more fine or pure, and can only be discerned by purer eyes. We cannot see it; but when our bodies are purified we shall see that it is all matter" (Doctrine and Covenants 131:7-8).

Traditional Christianity says that spirituality cannot be objectively proven; it must be accepted on faith alone. Additionally, many traditional Christian churches today say there are no revelations or miracles, but all of these things ended with the original Apostles of Jesus Christ.

Conversely, modern revelation teaches that when a person has spiritual experiences, that person moves beyond faith to knowledge. The Book of Mormon says, "And now, behold, is your knowledge perfect? Yea, your knowledge is perfect in that thing, and your faith is dormant" (Alma 32:34). Of course, you still need to exercise faith in things you have not yet experienced, "neither must ye lay aside your faith" (Alma 32:36).

We need to depend upon our faith, while gaining knowledge, until we are perfect. Modern revelation says, "That which is of God is light; and he that receiveth light, and continueth in God, receiveth more light; and that light groweth brighter and brighter until the perfect day" (Doctrine and Coventants 50:24). On the other hand, if we do not live according to the knowledge we have, we will lose that knowledge. As Jesus said in Matthew 13:12, "For whosoever hath, to him shall be given, and he shall have more abundance: but whosoever hath not, from him shall be taken away even that he hath."

Faith

Materialists scoff at faith and say that believing in anything unseen is irrational; however, we practice faith in unseen things every day. For example, when you drive a car, you have faith that if you stay on your side of the yellow lines, you will avoid a head-on collision. You have faith that drivers on the opposite side of the road will stay on their side of the yellow lines. How can yellow lines stop a car from crossing to your side of the road? They can't except by the power of faith. Another example is working. Why do you work for two weeks or a month without getting paid? It is because you have faith that you will be paid for your work at the next payday. Faith in God is no different.

More Refined Matter

Because spirit is more refined matter, we should be able to sense it through normal means or by machine. What we can sense is always increasing because of scientific progress. For example, if I had told you two hundred years ago that I could shine a light through your body and see your bones, you would have thought I was crazy. Now, X-rays are commonly accepted, as are infrared lights, ultraviolet lights, radio waves, and extremely low frequencies. Assumedly, there are many similar discoveries waiting to be made.

Over ninety-nine percent of the electromagnetic spectrum is invisible to the eye. We have discovered parts of this spectrum through experiments and machines. How much more of the electromagnetic spectrum is yet to be discovered?

Animals can sense things that humans cannot and vice-versa. If I blow a dog whistle, you won't hear anything, but all the dogs in the area will begin to bark. Dogs, however, don't see color.

Subliminal messages cannot normally be picked up by our senses, but studies show they still have a profound effect on us.

What if a spirit, though invisible to the human eye, can be observed on this spectrum by animals as well as cameras, recording devices, or other machines? What if a machine could be invented to observe spirits?

I believe humans will eventually invent machines to fight angels similar to the weapons in Ghostbusters (1984), but it won't be the weapons that repel the angels, it will be the attitude of the humans who wield them.

<u>Frequency</u>

The movie Dune (1984) showed the voice being used as a weapon. This could be symbolic of speaking up to combat injustice or silencing opposition to maintain power. However, the idea that noise can be a weapon is not just science fiction.

Legends say opera singers can shatter glass with their voices. Many people on social media have shared videos of themselves cracking glasses with their voices.

Sonic weapons have been used to cause headaches, dizziness, confusion, memory loss, distorted vision, nausea, bowel evacuation, and difficulty moving. They have been used against American ambassadors in foreign countries and various protestors.

Doppler Effect

The Doppler Effect describes how sound waves change with movement. When a car with a siren passes you, the sound drops because the sound waves take longer to reach your ears. The Doppler Effect works for light waves too. Stars in a telescope seem to have a red shift or a blue shift, depending on whether they are moving toward or away from the observer, respectively.

Atoms

Atoms are mostly spacious, but they contain positive and negative charges. When two solids come into contact with each other, they repel. If a person could reorganize the atoms of the body in such a way that those atoms would not be repelled by a solid, that person could theoretically move through solid objects.

John 20 tells about Jesus appearing twice in a room when the doors were shut. His apostles touched his body. Traditional Christians might explain this that Jesus could appear in alternating spirit or body. Since Jesus was resurrected and can never die again, which means His spirit can never leave His body again, His body must be able to move through solid objects.

Evil Influence

I saw a video of an abortion doctor telling an anti-abortion protester that he liked killing babies. He spoke gutturally, as if intentionally trying to be repulsive. (See Youtube, "Demon Possessed Abortion Doctor "I Love it!" (EVIL).)

I saw a video of a woman saying that she wanted to teach all little girls to be sluts to combat religion. She spoke like she was some powerful hypnotist attempting to mesmerize her audience. It didn't faze me.

Electronic Voice Phenomenon

The parents of a client of mine said they felt an evil spiritual presence in their son's bedroom, but could not see or hear anything. One evening, they left a recording device running for an hour or so—an idea they got from the "Ghost Hunters" television show. When they listened to it, they could hear a barely audible, creepy voice speaking.

If I told you that there are waves of sound flowing past you right now, you may not believe me, but if I turn on a radio and adjust the frequency, you could hear it clearly. What if there are "frequencies" of sound we have not discovered yet? What if spirituality is like a frequency? What if you have to tune your soul to receive divine guidance? You might tell me all you hear is static. I know because I heard static too before I got in tune.

Scientists say Extra-Sensory Perception, or ESP,

does not exist, but what about Extreme Sensory Perception, or senses in certain people that are more attuned than their peers? Some humans can sense things that others cannot. What scientific principle could explain this phenomenon?

<u>Windows of Learning</u>

Some people have highly attuned senses because of windows of learning in the developing brain. For example, Native Innuits have a hundred words for different kinds of snow. They teach their children to see different shades of ice to keep them from walking on thin ice. If you try to teach an adult how to see different shades of ice, it will all look the same because the adult's brain is already fully developed. Similarly, herders in Africa can see which cows are sick from the shade of their fur.

People with blindness from birth can't develop sight receptors in their brains. Doctors can repair their eyes, but their brains will not be able to capture images because when the brain is fully developed, the window of learning has passed.

What if there is a window of learning for spiritual matters? What if children raised in spiritual cultures or environments develop a greater capacity for perceiving spiritual matters than children from non-spiritual environments? I'm not saying this is true; I'm just raising the question.

Another explanation for why some people are more spiritually attuned than others is genes. What if there are genes that are more receptive to spiritual matters? What if certain genealogies are more spiritual than others?

The Church of Jesus Christ of Latter-day Saints teaches that we lived as spirits before we were born on earth. Babies being born with unique personalities appear to prove this. I personally believe—though it's not official Church doctrine—that I chose my parents and vice-versa. I believe I chose my family and lineage based on the spirits I was close to in the pre-existence. That my ancestors were spiritual is not a surprise to me.

Spiritual Growth

When a person grows spiritually, that person has greater awareness of good and evil, of God and the devil. When Moses saw Jesus Christ, he also saw the devil. (See Pearl of Great Price, Moses 1.) When a person grows closer to God, that person is more aware of sins, faults, and foibles. Furthermore, the more righteous a person becomes, the more potential for wickedness that person has. Jesus said; "for unto whomsoever much is given, of him shall be much required" (Luke 12:48). Jesus further said, "For of him unto whom much is given much is required; and he who sins against the greater light shall receive the greater condemnation" (Doctrine and Covenants 82:3). C. S. Lewis said, "The better stuff a creature is made of – the cleverer and stronger and freer it is – then the better it will be if it goes right, but also the worse it will be if it goes wrong" (See C.S. Lewis, Mere

Christianity, New York: Harper Collins, 1957, p. 48).

This was the case with Lucifer, a "son of the morning" (Isaiah 14:12). If he had followed Jesus Christ, he would have been a great force for good. Instead, he has become a great force for evil. He became Satan, the devil. When he fell from Heaven, he took a third of the spirits with him (See Revelations 12:4). Sons of Perdition are the same. (See Doctrine and Covenants 76:26, 32, and 43.) They could be forces for good. Instead, they choose to become forces for evil.

When the devil chose evil over good, the light and knowledge he had was taken from him. It was replaced with darkness and ignorance. The more evil he does, the more his ignorance grows.

If Oliver Cowdery had been faithful, he might have been in Hyrum Smith's place at Carthage Jail. If Thomas B. Marsh had been faithful, he might have led the Saints West in Brigham Young's place.

<u>Becoming Like God</u>

It is logical to me that puppies grow up to be dogs, kittens grow up to be cats, and children of God grow up to be like Him. Paul said, "Ye are the offspring of God" (Acs17:28-29). God wants us to be like Him. Jesus commanded, "Be ye therefore perfect, even as your Father which is in heaven is perfect" (Matthew 5:48). He wouldn't command something that we could not fulfill, albeit only through Him. Paul also said, "The Spirit itself beareth witness with our spirit, that we are the children of

God. And if children, then heirs; heirs of God, and joint-heirs with Christ; if so be that we suffer with him, that we may be also glorified together" (Romans 8:16-17). If we follow Jesus Christ, we will share in his inheritance of all that God has. If Jesus is God's heir then He is a God, and we can be joint-gods.

At Brigham Young University, I heard of allegations that members of the Church of Jesus Christ of Latter-day Saints worship Joseph Smith. While we admire Joseph Smith's role as the Prophet of the Restoration of the Church, we do not worship him as our Savior.

Sometimes, I think people are more critical of Church members because of our doctrine than they are of themselves. On my mission, a man said he couldn't agree with us believing that we could become gods. A short while later, he said his father adored his mother. I thought his choice of words was ironic; adore means to worship. Is it okay for a husband to adore his wife, but not for us to admire Joseph Smith? Joseph Smith revealed to us that our marriages didn't have to end at death but could continue time and for all eternity.

Steve Gardipee is a traditional Christian who died in Vietnam and came back. He said that when he died, God told him, "You will expand out into the cosmos and know all these things." He said he was given power and thought, "I'm a super-god, not disrespect for God, but I'm a super-god. We cannot comprehend what we're going to become." He felt like God was holding him in His two hands, like a baby and was proud of him, like a parent feels proud of a child when they're first born. God told him, "Even in this state as a super-god, you cannot begin to comprehend what I am." (See Youtube Life After Death Experience (NDE) with Steve Gardipee, Vietnam War Story / One of the Best NDEs.)

<u>Superstition</u>

One person's ancient and cherished belief is another person's folly and superstition. We all have beliefs that others would regard as superstitious. Even a belief in the efficacy of pure rationality and science could be regarded as superstitious in nature and practice. Many people treat Science as a religion.

Scientist Werner Heisenberg discussed religion with colleagues Paul Dirac and Wolfgang Pauli at Solvay Conference in 1927:

> Dirac said: "I cannot understand why we idle discussing religion. If we are honest – and as scientists, honesty is our precise duty – we cannot help but admit that any religion is a pack of false statements, deprived of any real foundation. The very idea of God is a product of human imagination. [...] I do not recognize any religious myth, at least because they contradict one another. [...]" Heisenberg's view was tolerant. Pauli had kept silent, after some initial remarks. But when finally he was asked for his opinion, jokingly he said: "Well, I'd say that also our friend Dirac has

got a religion and the first commandment of this religion is 'God does not exist and Paul Dirac is his prophet'". Everybody burst into laughter, including Dirac. (See Werner Heisenberg. 2007. Physics and Philosophy: The Revolution in Modern Science. HarperCollins.)

As humans, we tend to believe we are completely rational; however, studies show that we make decisions based on emotions then assign rational explanations to them. This makes people who own their own biases more self-accurate than the people who believe they are rational. People who pride themselves on being rational may actually be slightly more rational than the next person, but they, along with the rest of us humans, are more irrational than rational.

People have widely differing beliefs. Christians don't agree with Atheists. Furthermore, Christians don't even agree with other Christians, and Atheists don't even agree with other Atheists. I see questions on the Internet, such as "Do all women agree?" A more accurate question would be, "Can any two people agree completely?" The answer is *no*, and that's okay. People don't have to agree. They can agree to disagree. Not allowing disagreements is the hallmark of people obsessed with power and control.

I attended Brigham Young University as an undergraduate. I took a class from Hugh Nibley, a famous author in the Church of Jesus Christ of Latter-day Saints. He told me and the other students, "If I told you one tenth of what I believe, you would think I'm crazy. As it is, I've only told people one one-hundredth of what I believe, and they still think I'm crazy."

Spirituality

What is spirituality? It is belief in an unseen world, a world beyond our senses. It is part of our human nature. It is our true purpose in life.

Christians accept spirituality. If you believe in God, it follows that you believe in the devil. The Bible warns against evil spiritual practices, including "sorcery" (Acts 8:9), "curious arts" (Acts 19:19), "witchcraft" (Galatians 5:20), "sorceries" (Revelation 9:21 and 18:23), and "sorcerers" (Revelation 21:8). The Book of Mormon likewise warns against "sorceries, and witchcrafts, and magics" (Mormon 1:19) and "magic art, and the witchcraft which was in the land" (Mormon 2:10).

Curiosity about spiritual practices is natural. We are spiritual beings. I have learned to confine my study of spiritual phenomena to only what is good. Non-Christians who practice spirituality many times fall into evil spiritual practices. This is because they have no discernment to help them avoid these things.

Quantum Physics

The famous double-slit experiment showed that light behaves as a wave, but when it is observed, it behaves as a particle. Scientists have not yet discovered an explanation for this phenomenon.

Light as a wave can go through both slits; however, light as a particle goes only through one of the slits. Therefore, observation changes the nature of light from wave to particle. Isn't there a spiritual allegory here? God can do miracles, but when we want to prove the miracles, they lose their miraculous property. "But isn't God supposed to be all-powerful? Couldn't He do a miracle while we are watching?" asks the Atheist. Yes, of course, he is all-powerful, but just because He *could* do something doesn't mean he *should* do it. God wants us to have our freedom of choice. He doesn't want to take that away from us. Therefore, He will not openly display His power until the end of the world.

Hundreds of years ago, Hakuin Ekaku said, "Two hands clap and there is a sound. What is the sound of one hand?" Later, Western philosophers asked, "If a tree falls in a forest and no one is around to hear it, does it make a sound?"

Speed of Light

Science says nothing moves faster than the speed of light. The problem is, if something did, how would we know? We couldn't measure it, but that doesn't mean it doesn't exist. What if God moves faster than the speed of light? What if this is why we can't observe Him?

Atheism

I had a friend who said he was ninety-nine percent atheist and one percent believer. Knowing I was religious, he showed me some of his atheist literature. It encouraged agnostics to become atheists, and atheists to become "militant" atheists, attacking Christianity and the Bible. Why the push? Why not just say, "I don't know," and let Christianity and the Bible alone?

Agnosticism is a perfectly understandable position that there may be a god, there may not be, there's just no way to tell. It's much more defensible than the atheist position that there is no god in the universe. Really? How do you know? Have you traveled to every corner of the universe? If you can't even travel to every part of the earth in one lifetime, how much more impossible is it to travel to every part of the known universe? It stands to reason that there are parts of the universe that we don't know. Have you ever traveled beyond the known universe?

Atheists argue that there is no *objective* proof of God, and *subjective* proof is not enough. In other words, because they have not experienced God, no one else could have, and those who believe they have experienced God have only been fooled.

Furthermore, Atheists argue, all the suffering in the world today surely would have provoked God into revealing Himself objectively; however, God is not a puppet to be controlled by our behavior, whether good or bad. He does what He knows is best, not what we think He should do. God will reveal Himself to them eventually, but it will be on His terms, not theirs.

An ant crawled to the top of its ant hill and yelled, "If there is a gigantic foot in the world, let it come and step on me now." Nothing happened. The ant concluded, "I've proven that no giant foot exists!"

Plato taught that ideals exist independently of particulars, just as our idea of a tree exists independently of an imperfect tree. Another way to express this is that universals exist beyond particulars.

One definition of God is the most intelligent force in the Universe. According to that definition, Atheists would have to acknowledge admiring, if not worshipping someone, and most do admire various scientists, past and present. They could also call Nature or Chance "God" if they believe Nature or Chance rules the Universe.

C.S. Lewis talks about his conversion from Atheism, and says God stalked him in his quiet moments alone (Surprised By Joy, P. 266). He also called God "unscrupulous" (Surprised By Joy) because God doesn't play by human rules.

Joseph Smith told a member of the Church of Jesus Christ of Latter-day Saints, "When you joined this Church you enlisted to serve God. When you did that you left the neutral ground, and you can never get back to it. Should you forsake the Master you enlisted to serve it will be by the instigation of the evil one, and you will follow his dictation and be his servant" (Recollections of the Prophet Joseph Smith, The Juvenile Instructor, Vol. XXVIII, No. 16).

The Shroud of Turin

The Shroud of Turin is a microcosm of the clash between science and religion. The Shroud contains an image of a man who was whipped, crowned with thorns, crucified, and stabbed in the side. The man was buried according to Jewish Custom at the time of Jesus Christ. According to scientists, rigor mortus set in while the man was crucified. Afterwards, he was washed. The Shroud contains anointing oil, flowers, pollen, and dirt particles from Jerusalem at the time of Jesus Christ as well as pollen from Constantinople in the 13th Century. Believing scientists find this evidence compelling.

Mainstream scientists have found contradicting evidence to almost every aspect of the Shroud of Turin. Some of their research follows.

The mainstream scientific view of the Shroud of Turin is that it was the product of 13th Century Medieval artists. One artist even confessed to painting it. The problem is that it was not painted.

Mainstream scientists argue that the Shroud of Turin matches, detail for detail, every painting, statue, and mosaic in Constantinople around the 13th Century. They view this as evidence that the Shroud of Turin was created by the same artists that created all the other religious iconography from that time period and area. Conversely, religious scientists argue that all of the religious iconography in Constantinople in the 13th Century was copied from the Shroud of Turin because it was the held to be authentic.

Shallow Science

No amount of experimentation can ever prove me right; a single experiment can prove me wrong—Albert Einstein

The problem with science is contradictory evidence. Faced with contradictory evidence most scientists and non-scientists jump to a conclusion based on their biases. However, not all evidence is equal.

If one scientist studies the Shroud of Turin for twelve years and another scientist studies it for five minutes, wouldn't it be intellectually honest to give more weight to the first scientist's evidence regardless of the findings?

In the case of the Shroud of Turin, the main evidence against the Shroud is Radiocarbon Dating.

Shallow Science is when people do the bare minimum research to find one piece of evidence to support their theory then dismiss all evidence to the contrary. It is like confirmation bias, but with the false sense of scientific proof to back it up.

One of my clients in California said, "I tried Jesus. It didn't work." First, Jesus is a "He," not an "It." Second, how long did my client "try" Jesus, fifteen minutes? My client used drugs for fifteen years. He should have given Jesus at least that long of a trial!

Radiocarbon Dating

The Shroud of Turin has been dated to around the

13th Century with 95% accuracy. However, is radiocarbon dating infallible? Is it the best method for testing age?

Radiocarbon Dating is not infallible, including the percent of accuracy it claims. For proof of this, look to Radiometric Dating. Radiometric Dating estimates that the earth is over four and a half billion years old. It estimates that the Tyrannosaurus Rex lived 66 million or more years ago. Then in 2005, a Tyrannosaurus Rex was found with soft tissue still intact. Did that change the Mainstream Scientific view on the age of dinosaurs? No! They simply found ways to argue how the soft tissue was preserved for billions of years. Occam's razor grew dull in this situation!

The Shroud of Turin has been dated to the time of Jesus Christ by Infrared Light and Spectroscopy. These techniques were not available at the time the Shroud was first tested. They are newer and more accurate than Radiocarbon Dating. However, Mainstream Science still considers this contradictory evidence as less weighty than the former Radiocarbon Dating. Likewise, many media outlets report the Radiocarbon Dating more than the Infrared Light and Spectroscopy Dating.

Occam's Razor

Scientists use Occam's razor to dismiss Creationism; however, I see Occam's Razor as supporting Creationism. Let's perform a thought experiment. You roll six dice and try to get each to land on a different number, one through six. Count how many tries it would take you. Meanwhile, I'll take six dice and arrange them one through six. This is the difference between chance and creation. They're both *possible,* but one is many times more *probable.*

You could wait a lifetime for a book to be written by chance, or you could write one. The idea that this world took billions of years to come into being is much more miraculous to me than that God had created it.

The view that Joseph Smith wrote the Book of Mormon is more miraculous to me than if he translated it by the power of God. To write the Book of Mormon, Joseph would have had to be a genius greater than all the great authors in the history of the world. The view that Joseph wrote the Book of Mormon by the power of the devil is a more understandable view in my mind than that he wrote it himself; however, the devil can't create good, he can only taint it and make it evil.

Higher Law

Sir Isaac Newton created a Theory of Gravity in the 17th Century. Einstein gave a more correct Theory of Gravity in modern times. Does this mean that Newton's Theory is incorrect? If so, then so is Einstein's! Just as Einstein's Theory is more correct than Newton's, so Newton's is more correct than others. Even the theory that the earth was flat was better than no theory at all.

In the same way, Jesus said, "Ye have heard that it was said by them of old time, Thou shalt not commit adultery: but I say unto you, That whosoever looketh upon a woman to lust after her hath committed adultery with her already in his heart" (Matthew 5:27-28). Jesus gave a higher law than the Ten Commandments. This doesn't mean the Ten Commandments were wrong or that we no longer have to follow them. If we follow the higher law, it is given that we also follow the Ten Commandments. Likewise, wouldn't it make sense that Jesus continues to give us higher and higher laws as we are ready to accept them, until we are perfect?

Mainstream Science

Mainstream Science claims to be the most correct view known to humans. It decides what is most correct. All other types of science are deemed "Fringe Science."

What makes Science mainstream? Is it the view accepted by the most scientists? Is it the view backed by most experts in that field of study? Is it the least complex view? Is it the view backed by rich and politically connected people? If governing bodies award money to certain fields of study or certain types of study, wouldn't it follow that the majority of scientists would gravitate towards those fields and types of study? Does that mean that other fields or types of study are not worth studying?

What if Mainstream Science declares something to be true even if it is false? Does that mean that non-scientists must accept it because they are not "experts"? Does it mean those who don't accept it are against Science itself?

Proofs of God

Have you ever thought about how the sun and moon look about the same size in the sky? First, the earth had to be far enough from the sun to be cool, but close enough to be warm. Then, the moon had to be far enough from the earth not to run into it, but close enough to not drift away. God went to a lot of trouble to arrange all this! Don't take it for granted.

I saw a video—I don't remember the name—about how the Earth lies at the end of one of the arms of the Milky Way Galaxy. If it were closer to the middle of the galaxy, we wouldn't be able to see much of the universe around us. Earth is on the inside of the arm. If it were on the outside, it would be destroyed by meteorites. It's as if God wanted us to see as much of His creation as possible while still being relatively safe.

<u>Jesus Proves that God Lives</u>

Some people deny that Jesus lived. There is as much proof that Jesus lived as any person in history. People who deny this proof have to ask themselves if they are truly being honest.

Some people deny that Jesus was the Son of God. They say He was human, just like the rest of us. C. S. Lewis, in his book, Mere Christianity, said it best:

Either this man was, and is, the Son of God, or else a madman or something worse. You can shut him up for a fool, you can spit at him and kill him as a demon or you can fall at his feet and call him Lord and God, but let us not come with any patronizing nonsense about his being a great human teacher. He has not left that open to us. He did not intend to.

Jesus said He was the Son of God. He was put to death for blasphemy, though ironically, He could not commit blasphemy. People demand more proof. So God has given them more

The Bible Proves that God Lives

Once upon a time, a group of children lived in a house without parents. The older children had dim memories of their parents. The younger children had no memories of their parents. One of the younger children misbehaved. One of the older children corrected the younger child. "That's wrong," said the older child.

"Says who?", asks the younger child.

"Our parents."

"What parents?"

"Our parents," said the older child.

"I don't know any parents," said the younger child.

"They built this house."

"So you say."

"I saw them. They lived with us."

"So you say again. I think you're trying to fool us."

"No, I'm not. Look, here's a letter from them." The older child shows the younger child a letter.

"That's not from them. You wrote that."

"This letter is too complicated for me to write."

"You or another child wrote it."

"Our parents are coming back."

"When?"

"Soon."

"I don't believe you. I think you just want to tell me what to do. I don't have to listen to you. There are no parents."

So act atheists. The Bible is God's letter to us, His children. It is much too complicated for humans to write. Just look at Jesus' Sermon on the Mount. The great Shakespeare doesn't even come close to it!

On a side note, many atheists argue that in an almost infinite universe, our world came into being by chance. You could make the same argument about a dictionary or Shakespeare's plays. If this is true, reading Shakespeare is no better or worse than reading a dictionary or a random list of letters!

The Bible has been the most attacked book throughout the history of the world. First, historical religious leaders "have taken away from the gospel of the Lamb many parts which are plain and most precious; and also many covenants of the Lord have they taken away" (1 Nephi 13:26). Second, they banned the Bible from common use. Third, they prevented it from being translated into common speech. Their efforts have failed, and the Bible is spreading across the world. Now, the devil has changed tactics. When he can't suppress the Bible, he ridicules it and calls it irrelevant.

What amazes me about the Bible is how a book written between two and four thousand years ago can be so accurate today!

Atheists denounce the Bible as a Fairy Tale. They demand more proof. So God has given them more proof.

Israel Proves that God Lives

Israel has survived miraculously despite the world's best efforts to destroy Israel. Even today, many nations want to destroy Israel. One day, these nations will gather their armies together and march against Israel. They will fail as all people have failed in the past.

I argued with an atheist who was a former minister that Israel is proof that God lives. He said Israel has such an influence on the world as to make us believe that they have survived miraculously when they have only survived through human ingenuity. To me, that would be a greater miracle than Israel surviving through divine intervention!

Judeo-Christian Values

Jared Diamond, in his book, "Guns, Germs, and Steel," puts forth compelling reasons why some societies have dominated others throughout history. Some of these are milking cows for food instead of killing them, living in temperate agricultural zones, spreading crops in a latitudinal direction, experiencing large population growths, developing immunity to diseases, and discovering scientific inventions. His book received several awards. Conversely, morality was his blind spot. For example, he talked about a primitive tribe that accepts men having sex with goats, but he doesn't talk about how that behavior weakened and held back the tribe. (See Jared Diamond, 1997, "Guns, Germs, and Steel: The Fates of Human Societies," W.W. Norton and Co. Inc.: New York.)

Diamond and I agree that no one group of people is better than another. He says secular reasons are why some societies flourished. I see history as proof that Judeo-Christian values gave some societies advantage over others, and the closer those societies lived Judeo-Christian values, the more advantage they had. The opposite was also true. When a blessed people sinned against a greater light, they had a greater condemnation (See Doctrine and Covenants 82:3).

The Book of Jasher portrays the people of Sodom and Gomorrah as a Covenant People. In other words, they promised their lives to the Lord. This may have been why the Lord was so harsh with them as opposed to other peoples around them at the same time.

Sometimes, the Lord spares wicked cities due to the presence of a few righteous people. Abraham asked the Lord to spare the cities of Sodom and Gomorrah. The Lord promised to do so even if He found ten righteous people (Genesis 18:32). He did find one righteous person, Lot, whom he warned to escape before He destroyed the cities.

The ancient Egyptians were one of the earliest empires. At one time they were the most powerful empire in the world.

The Israelites left Egypt and conquered Canaan. In the Book of Mormon, Nephi tells Laman and Lemuel that the Israelites would not have gained the promised land if they hadn't been more righteous than the Canaanites (See 1 Nephi 17: 33-34). Nephi tells them how the Lord deals with nations, "And he raiseth up a righteous nation, and destroyeth the nations of the wicked" (1 Nephi 17:37).

Israel under King Solomon became the richest and most powerful kingdom on earth. Because of wickedness, Ten Tribes of the Kingdom of Israel split off from the Kingdom of Judah. Then, the Assyrians conquered Egypt and the Ten Tribes of the Kingdom of Israel. The Ten Tribes were at least as wicked as the Assyrians. As Covenant People, the Ten Tribes would have been under great condemnation because they were sinning against a greater light.

I used to mourn for the Ten Tribes when they were conquered by the Assyrians. Then, I read about their moral condition in the Old Testament, how they worshipped false gods with feasts and orgies, and then burned the babies that were born as sacrifices to the false gods. I felt sick and said, "Lord, destroy them and scatter them!" even though they were my own ancestors.

Not all of them were evil. The Lord told Elijah, "Yet I have left me seen thousand in Israel, all the knees which have not bowed unto Baal, and every mouth which hath not kissed him" (1 Kings 19:18). Sometimes, the righteous are punished with the wicked. The Lord likely spared the lives of the more righteous part of the people and they escaped to the Kingdom of Judah or were taken as slaves by the Assyrians.

The Kingdom of Judah also became wicked. They were conquered by the Babylonians. The King of Babylon, Nebuchadnezzar, was wicked, but he repented and praised God. When he died, his son, Belshazzar, became King. Belshazzar had a feast and drank from the cups of the Temple of Solomon. The Lord wrote his doom on the wall. He was killed, and Babylon was conquered by the Persians.

The Greeks conquered Media-Persia. The Romans conquered many lands, including Greece, the Kingdom of Judah, and Britain. The Romans were able to conquer the Kingdom of Judah because it had become wicked and sinned against the greater light.

Next, the Anglo-Saxons conquered Britain. They were converted to Christianity and became righteous in many ways. When King Ethelred was caught with a woman, they were married, and she became Queen of England.

The Anglo-Saxon Chronicle was written by Church leaders. It praises the righteous acts by the King and condemns the wicked ones, like the slaying of King Edward, "There has not been 'mid Angles / a worse deed done / than this was, / since they first / Britain-land sought" (See Anglo-Saxon Chronicle, AD 979). It recounts how the leaders led the people in righteousness and wickedness. The tone sounds a lot like the Old Testament and the Book of Mormon.

The Anglo-Saxons became corrupt and stopped living Judeo-Christian values. They were conquered by the Vikings. King Canute the Great became King. His Anglo-Saxon courtiers said he was so great, even the sea would obey him. He decided to teach them a lesson. He placed his throne in front of a rising tide and commanded the waves to stay back. When his feet got wet, he told the courtiers that only God can command the sea.

Next, the Anglo-Saxons were conquered by the Normans. Eventually, the Welsh united with the Normans to form Great Britain. After that, the Scottish united with the British to form the United Kingdom. The Puritans and Pilgrims left the United Kingdom and came to the United States of America (USA). Now the USA is the most powerful country on earth.

Throughout history, blessed nations have become corrupt. The writers of the Bible and Book of Mormon especially seem to emphasize this theme, over and over again. They are trying to warn us from making the same mistakes, though we all do. When Judeo-Christian societies become wicked, they fall from God's favor and become like the other nations around them. (See 1 Samuel 8:20.)

I once saw an award-winning book about the Civil War. I can't remember the title or author. The author said he removed references to God because people back then talked in a more flowery and poetic way than now. To me, that seemed like an excuse. Do we dismiss our forbearers' deeply religious beliefs as mere superstition? Does our secular society feel uncomfortable with frequent references to God? Do we censor frequent references to God or ban it outright because of our disbelief?

Freedom of Religion guaranteed by the United States Constitution broke the hold of false religions on politics. However, when Jesus comes again, He won't give us a democratic republic; He will give us His Kingdom.

We modern humans are used to secular societies. We have lived so long without religious-based governments that we don't understand them. Even in Europe, where religion and government comingle, the society has become more secular than not. The government has become more influential than religion. Before the separation of Church and State, all governments were more or less religious. We look at history as secular because we have a secular point of view. To understand our forerunners, we have to look at the religion that was such a part of their lives.

Side Notes of History

I once read an Encyclopedia that had an article on early religious revival in America. It had Joseph Smith's story in a side note. I thought it was ironic that the founding of the most important American religion had been relegated to a side note! Likewise, I found that in the same Encyclopedia, there was an article on the Hundred Years War, and Joan of Arc had been relegated to a side note. At least Joseph Smith was in good company!

I wonder if Jesus Christ Himself will be relegated to a side note in future history books! He might be now if His influence wasn't so prevalent. As Nephi wrote, "Even the God of Israel do men trample under their feet but I would speak in other words – they set him at naught, and hearken not to the voice of his counsels" (2 Nephi 19:7).

Islam

I heard that Muslims are more religious than Christians. If you take the average Muslim and average Christian, it might be true. That doesn't mean that Islam is more correct than Christianity.

Part of the reason Muslims are so religious is that they have no separation of Church and State. Modern Christians have difficulty understanding that concept. That is also why the Old Testament was so strict. The ancient Jews had no separation of Church and State. Neither did the ancient Christians. When you broke a religious law, you also broke a government law, and you could be punished severely for it.

Modern Christianity is much more tolerant of sin than modern Islam. Muslims remind us Christians to take our Christianity more seriously.

In the Book of Mormon, whenever the Nephites became lazy in their worship, the Lamanites gained power over them. The Lord told Nephi that the Lamanites "shall be a scourge unto thy seed, to stir them up in the ways of remembrance" (1 Nephi 2:24). The United States of America, as a whole, is turning away from Christianity, and Islam is gaining power over our Country. Maybe this is the Lord's way of reminding us to turn to Him for salvation, both temporal and spiritual.

United Order

The early members of the Church of Jesus Christ of Latter-day Saints practiced the United Order, or having all things in common. Many who lived this way said it was the happiest time of their lives. Regrettably, the Saints weren't able to live this way for long. Selfishness took hold, and these communities eventually broke apart.

Some of the communities who practiced the United Order under Brigham Young were more successful and wealthy than the surrounding communities.

I heard that Orderville was one of the last communities to practice the United Order. One teenaged boy saved wool from sheep tails and bought a pair of pants outside the order. The leaders commended him for his enterprise, offered to use his pants as a pattern for all pants, and promised him the first pair. Regrettably, his act led to other breaks with the order, which ultimately ended it.

After Jesus Christ visited the Nephites and Lamanites in the Book of Mormon, they were all converted to Him, and they lived in a communal society for two centuries. Expensive clothes were one of the first signs of apostasy among these Saints. "And now, in this two hundred and first year there began to be among them those who were lifted up in pride, such as the wearing of costly apparel, and all manner of fine pearls, and of the fine things of the world. And from that time forth they did have their goods and their substance no more common among them" (4 Nephi 1:24-25). This apostasy ultimately led to the destruction of the Nephites, and the dwindling of the Lamanites in unbelief until the latter days.

Historians

At some point among historians, it became fashionable to deny anything that was not found in a primary source written at the time of the event. Although this approach is helpful, it can be counter-productive when it is taken to the extreme.

For example, a spiritual phenomenon known as Brigham Young's transfiguration occurred on August 8, 1844. Brigham Young gave a speech where he looked and sounded like the late Joseph Smith. Modern historians say that this spiritual phenomenon was only the product of "contagious" thought or "collective memory" that was only written down later.

Did everyone present witness the transfiguration? I doubt it. It was probably given as a sign to the faithful. Also, some *saw* Joseph's likeness. Others *heard* his voice. This is consistent with Paul's definition of various gifts of the spirit (See 1 Corinthians 12:4-10). We have spiritual gifts based on our talents. We must develop them with practice. No imperfect human has likely had *all* spiritual gifts at once. Though not all present witnessed the same things and maybe some witnessed nothing at all, all present sustained Brigham Young's leadership.

My great-great-grandfather, Arza Hinckley, was present at the meeting. Years later, he wrote about it in a letter to his daughter. Why didn't he write about it sooner? Maybe, he didn't have an audience. Maybe, he, like Mary, felt it was too sacred to share; "But Mary kept all these things, and pondered them in her heart" (Luke 2:19). Maybe, he was being modest. Arza's daughter asked him why he didn't talk about his role in the rescue of the Martin handcart company, as he was second into the camp and helped Ephraim Hanks administer to the people. He said he preferred to let others have the credit.

Should I believe skeptical historian deniers or should I believe my own great-great grandfather?

Unfortunately for historical deniers, first-hand accounts written at the time of Brigham Young's transfiguration were discovered. This didn't convince them, however. Skeptics will always argue. If you resolve one point, they will raise another, and so on into eternity.

Like the historians that deny Brigham Young's transfiguration, a twenty-something-year-old denied the Miracle at KapYong, where 240 Utah National Guardsmen fought 4000 Chinese, and survived. I saw a documentary in which Chinese soldiers testified that they repeatedly shot the Guardsmen, but the Guardsmen did not fall down. Who should I believe—an historian who was not even born until after the Korean War, or enemy eye-witnesses who have no reason to lie?

Jesus

God wanted His Prophets in the Old Testament to write about Jesus Christ, but God knew the devil would destroy direct references to Jesus Christ in the Old Testament. God left signs in the Old Testament about Jesus Christ that are plain to Christians, but not to others. The most famous of these are the following:

Isaiah 7:14, "Therefore, the Lord himself shall give you a sign—Behold, a virgin shall conceive, and shall bear a son, and shall call his name Immanuel."

Isaiah 9:6, "For unto us a child is born, unto us a son is given: and the government shall be upon his shoulder: and his name shall be called Wonderful, Counsellor, The mighty God, The everlasting Father, The Prince of Peace."

Isaiah 53: 5, "But he was wounded for our transgressions, he was bruised for our iniquities: the chastisement of our peace was upon him; and with his stripes we are healed."

The Church of Jesus Christ of Latter-day Saints

Similarly, God left signs in the Bible about modern revelation that are plain to members of the Church of Jesus Christ of Latter-day Saints, but not to others.

Leviticus 10:9, speaking to Aaron, says, "Do not drink wine nor strong drink, thou, nor thy sons with thee, when ye go into the tabernacle of the congregation, lest ye die; it shall be a statue forever throughout your generations." This is a sign of the modern day Word of Wisdom, and the modern sons of Aaron, or those who accept the Aaronic Priesthood.

John 10:16 says, "Other sheep I have, which are not of this fold: them also I must bring, and they shall hear my voice; and there shall be one fold, and one shepherd." This is a sign of Jesus Christ appearing to the Nephites and Lamanites in Ancient America.

Isaiah 2:2–3 says the following:

> And it shall come to pass in the last days, that the mountain of the Lord's house shall be established in the top of the mountains, and shall be exalted above the hills; and all nations shall flow unto it. And many people shall go up and say, Come ye, and let us go up to the mountain of the Lord, to the house of the God of Jacob; and he will teach us of his ways, and we will walk in his paths: for out of Zion shall go forth the law, and the word of the Lord from Jerusalem.

This is a sign of the Church of Jesus Christ of Latter-day Saints being based in the Rocky Mountains.

Isaiah 29:4 says, "And thou shalt be brought down, and shalt speak out of the ground, and thy speech shall be low out of the dust, and thy voice shall be, as of one that hath a familiar spirit, out of the ground, and thy speech shall whisper out of the dust." This is a sign of the Book of

Mormon being translated in the latter days.

Isaiah 29:11-12 says, "And the vision of all is become unto you as the words of a book that is sealed, which men deliver to one that is learned, saying, Read this, I pray thee: and he saith, I cannot; for it is sealed: And the book is delivered to him that is not learned, saying Read this, I pray thee: and he saith, I am not learned." This is a sign of Martin Harris delivering Book of Mormon script to Charles Anthon.

Isaiah 29: 14 says, "Therefore, behold, I will proceed to do a marvelous work among this people, even a marvelous work and a wonder." This is a sign of the restoration of the true Church of Jesus Christ.

Jeremiah 23:7-8 says, "Therefore, behold the days come, saith the Lord, that they shall no more say, The Lord liveth, which brought up the children of Israel out of the land of Egypt; But the Lord liveth, which brought up and which led the seed of the house of Israel out of the north country, and from all the countries whither I had driven them; and they shall dwell in their own land." This is a sign of the gathering of Israel in the last days.

Jeremiah 16:16 says, "Behold, I will send for many fishers, saith the Lord, and they shall fish them; and after will I send for many hunters, and they shall hunt them from every mountain, and from every hill, and out of the holes of the rocks." This is a sign of the organized missionary work of the Church of Jesus Christ of Latter-day Saints.

Ezekiel 37: 16-17 says, "Moreover, thou son of

man, take thee one stick and write upon it, For Judah, and for the children of Israel his companions: then take another stick, and write upon it, For Joseph, the stick of Ephraim, and for all the house of Israel his companions: And join them one to another into one stick; and they shall become one in thine hand." This is a sign of the Bible and the Book of Mormon becoming one in the last days.

<u>Non-Biblical Signs</u>

Signs are not limited to the Bible. There are many signs in traditional Jewish and Christian religious writings.

Jewish legends, including the Book of Enoch, say that Rachel, Joseph's mother, prophesied of "Messiah Ben Joseph (Messiah Son of Joseph)." He will live in the "last days." He will be a descendant of Ephraim. He will be the forerunner of Messiah Ben David—Jesus Christ. He will reveal true faith after a period of apostasy. The Prophet, Elijah, will appear to him. He will rebuild the Temple of Israel. He will gather many of the children of Israel, including from the Lost Ten Tribes. He will be a warrior. He will be a leader. He will die as a martyr. This is a sign of Joseph Smith and his life.

Ode 23 of The Odes of Solomon talks about a letter sent from God, many hands rushed to seize it, but they could not because the power of the seal was greater than they, it was received by the Kingdom, the Kingdom overcame much, "and the letter was a great volume, which was wholly written by the finger of God" (19). This is a sign of the Book of Mormon being translated by the power of God.

The law of fasting was revealed to the Shepherd of Hermas, who Paul may have mentioned in Romans 16:4, "Thus therefore do. Having performed what is before written, that day on which thou fastest thou shalt taste nothing at all but bread and water; and computing the quantity of food which thou art wont to eat upon other days, thou shalt lay aside the expense which thou shouldest have made that day, and give it unto the widow, the fatherless, and the poor (5:30). This is a sign of the modern day fast offerings.

Coincidence

Believers see signs in events all around them. Skeptics see only coincidence. For example, Joseph Smith prophesied about the Civil War, including where it would begin (See Doctrine and Covenants 87). At the time, he was laughed at. How much suffering could have been averted if people had listened to him?

President Gordon B. Hinckley read "The Family: A Proclamation to the World" to the Relief Society on September 23, 1995, including "marriage between a man and a woman is ordained of God." New definitions of marriage had been proposed in 1993 in Hawaii. Until this time, traditional marriage had been the common definition accepted for thousands of years. The First Presidency could have viewed this as a passing fad, but they viewed it as the beginning of major changes in society. Why did they feel the need to define marriage in a proclamation to the world? Was this a coincidence?

I personally went door to door with several companions in California, arguing in favor of Proposition 8. At one door, one of my companions told a woman that if Proposition 8 failed, schools would be mandated to teach gay marriage. She said she didn't believe it. I testify that even before the vote came, high schools, middle schools, and even elementary schools began teaching gay marriage. There was also a bill before the State Congress to mandate it.

Likewise, the First Presidency wrote, "Gender is an essential characteristic of individual premortal, mortal, and eternal identity and purpose." Did they know there would be over a hundred genders by the 2000s?

President Hinckley spoke in October 1998 about Pharaoh's Dream in Genesis 41, including the seven years of plenty before the famine. He talked about how fragile the economy can be, and how it could affect us individuals. He said he was not prophesying, but he advised us to get our houses in order. In October 2001, he said, "I cannot forget the great lesson of Pharaoh's Dream of the fat and lean kine and of the full and withered stalks of corn." This time, there was no disclaimer about not prophesying. In October 2008, exactly seven years later, the economy crashed. Was this a coincidence?

Russell M. Nelson, President of the Church of Jesus Christ of Latter-day Saints, is a famous heart surgeon. He emphasized a home-centered Church. Soon afterwards, the Coronavirus became a pandemic. All Church meetings were canceled. Was it a coincidence that President Nelson encouraged Church members to worship in their homes just before Church meetings were canceled? Is it a coincidence that the Coronavirus came along when the President of the Church was a doctor?

Right after Church meetings were canceled due to the Coronavirus, an earthquake damaged the Salt Lake Temple, knocking the trumpet out of the hands of the Statue Moroni on top. How could members of the Church not see this as a sign? As the Lord says in Doctrine and Covenants 43:25, as follows:

> How oft have I called upon you by the mouth of my servants, and by the ministering of angels, and by mine own voice, and by the voice of thunderings, and by the voice of lightnings, and by the voice of tempests, and by the voice of earthquakes, and great hailstorms, and by the voice of famines and pestilences of every kind, and by the great sound of a trump, and by the voice of judgment, and by the voice of mercy all the day long, and by the voice of glory and honor and the riches of eternal life, and would have saved you with an everlasting salvation, but ye would not!

The Constancy of the Church of Jesus Christ of Latter-day Saints

The Church of Jesus Christ of Latter-day Saints was

restored on April 6, 1830. Most Protestant churches were about three hundred years older. The Church was referred to as a "new" church; however, it doesn't seem so new now.

Joseph Smith wrote the Articles of Faith before March 1842. Although many restored Church practices have changed, these articles of doctrine have not. In contrast, many Protestant churches have changed their doctrines in major ways. For example, many Baptist churches that were founded on baptism by immersion, no longer consider baptism necessary for salvation. Likewise, many Protestant churches accept that members of other Protestant churches are going to Heaven. This was not the case in the early 1900s when the Presbyterians condemned the Methodists to hell and vice-versa according to literature of the day (See L.M. Montgomery, "Anne's House of Dreams," Chapter 8).

Joseph Smith wrote, "Thus came the voice of the Lord unto me, saying: All who have died without a knowledge of this gospel, who would have received it if they had been permitted to tarry, shall be heirs of the celestial kingdom of God; Also all that shall die henceforth without a knowledge of it, who would have received it with all their hearts, shall be heirs of that kingdom" (Doctrine and Covenants 137:7-8). In the early 1900s, this doctrine found its way into Protestant churches, sometimes causing a stir. According to contemporary literature, a new Presbyterian minister "says he doesn't believe all the heathen will be eternally lost (L.M.

Montgomery, "Anne of the Island," Chapter V). Two authors ask if this and other Protestant doctrines changed because of Joseph Smith (David L. Paulsen and Hal R. Boyd, 2017, "Are Christians Mormon?" Routledge, Taylor and Francis Group: London and New York).

The Book of Mormon Clarifies Doctrine

In 3 Nephi 11:33, Jesus says, "And whoso believeth in me, and is baptized, the same shall be saved; and they are they who shall inherit the kingdom of God. And whoso believeth not in me, and is not baptized, shall be damned." This confirms what Jesus said in Mark 16:16, "He that believeth and is baptized shall be saved; but he that believeth not shall be damned."

Isaiah 7:14 says, "Therefore the Lord himself shall give you a sign; Behold, a virgin shall conceive, and bear a son, and shall call his name Immanuel." Some scholars argue that the word "virgin" here should be translated "young woman," and that this mistranslation is what gave rise to the doctrine that Jesus Christ was conceived by a virgin. 2 Nephi 17 translates this word, "virgin," confirming the doctrine. If God had wanted Joseph Smith to translate the word as "young woman," He would have had Joseph Smith do so.

The Book of Mormon Testifies that the Bible is True

Nephi writes about an angel showing him the future. He sees Bibles in America. Then he sees copies of the Book of Mormon in America. He writes, "And the angel spake unto me, saying: These last records, which thou hast seen among the Gentiles [copies of the Book of Mormon], shall establish the truth of the first, which are of the twelve apostles of the Lamb [Bibles], and shall make known the plain and precious things which have been taken away from them" (1 Nephi 13:40).

Later, Mormon writes to his descendants about the Book of Mormon and the Bible, "Lay hold upon the Gospel of Christ, which shall be set before you, not only in this record [the Book of Mormon] but also in the record which shall come unto the Gentiles from the Jews [the Bible], which record shall come from the Gentiles unto you. For behold this [the Book of Mormon] is written for the intent that ye may believe that [the Bible]" (Mormon 7:8–9). He continues, "And if ye believe that [the Bible] ye will believe this also [the Book of Mormon]" (Mormon 7:9).

Common Spiritual Experiences

People experience the Holy Ghost in different ways. Some people are confused that Heavenly Father has not caused their "bosom to burn" (Doctrine and Covenants 9:8) as He told Oliver Cowdery, but that revelation was given specifically to Oliver and does not necessarily apply to other people.

I love sailboats. One reason I love them is I feel Heavenly Father's presence in the wind. You would think that I love flying, but I don't. I don't particularly like motorboats either. I'm a good swimmer. I like attempting to surf and playing in the ocean, but there is something about sailing that inspires me.

When I attended the open house of the Oquirrh Mountain Temple, we watched a short video in a tent pavilion in the parking lot. As we prepared to go into the Temple, a gust of wind blew through the pavilion and rattled some of the technological equipment. It reminded me of wind chimes, which I love. It was as if Heavenly Father was saying, "Hello."

Instinct

Instinct is perception based solidly in the five senses. It is immediate and subtle, so it may seem to be an extra sense, but it is not.

Intuition

Intuition is similar to instinct, but is not based solidly in the five senses. It relies more on mental contemplation or meditation. A common definition of intuition is to know things automatically without having to test them out. Intuition could be described as a gut feeling that something is wrong. For example, a mother may intuitively know what is wrong with her child without knowing how she knows.

Inspiration

Inspiration is a divine prompting guiding us in our actions. The Holy Ghost prompts us to remember scriptures we've read and experiences we've had. Jesus said, "But the Comforter, which is the Holy Ghost, whom the Father will send in my name, he shall teach you all things, and bring all things to your remembrance, whatsoever I have said unto you" (John 14:26). So many times, our thoughts and memories are prompted by inspiration.

A good example of inspired promptings and how they work with our own thoughts is recorded by Nephi in the Book of Mormon when he was prompted to kill Laban. Nephi is very clear about the promptings of the Holy Ghost and his own thoughts. "And it came to pass that I was constrained by the Spirit that I should kill Laban" (1 Nephi 4:10). This was a prompting from the Holy Ghost.

"But I said in my heart: Never at any time have I shed the blood of man. And I shrunk and would that I might not slay him" (1 Nephi 4:10). These were Nephi's own thoughts and actions.

"And the Spirit said unto me again: Behold the Lord hath delivered him into thy hands" (1 Nephi 4:11). This was another prompting.

"Yea, and I also knew that he had sought to take away mine own life; yea, and he would not hearken unto the commandments of the Lord; and he also had taken away our property" (1 Nephi 4:11). These were three of Nephi's memories inspired by the Holy Ghost.

"And it came to pass that the Spirit said unto me again: Slay him, for the Lord hath delivered him into thy hands; Behold the Lord slayeth the wicked to bring forth his righteous purposes. It is better that one man should perish than that a nation should dwindle and perish in unbelief" (1 Nephi 4:12-13). This is a prompting of the Holy Ghost which included reasoning. Sometimes the Lord reasons with us as a man would, or in other words, speaks to us at our level of understanding (See Doctrine and Covenants 50:11).

"And now, when I, Nephi, had heard these words, I remembered the words of the Lord which he spake unto me in the wilderness, saying that: Inasmuch as thy seed shall keep my commandments, they shall prosper in the land of promise" (1 Nephi 4:14). This is another inspired memory.

> Yea, and I also thought that they could not keep the commandments of the Lord according to the law of Moses, save they should have the law. And I also knew that the law was engraven upon the plates of brass. And again, I knew that the Lord had delivered Laban into my hands for this cause—that I might obtain the records according to his commandments (1 Nephi 4:15-17)

These are Nephi's thoughts and reasoning on the promptings that he had received. Doubtless these thoughts and reasons were also inspired by the Holy Ghost as Heavenly Father was teaching Nephi to think like Himself.

Nephi didn't want to kill Laban. Ironically, one way I know I am receiving a prompting from the Holy Ghost is when it goes against my own will. Once, I applied for a job in Riverside, California. I didn't get the job, but they told me they liked my interview, and they had more openings coming up. I was excited about it. The next morning, I woke up and knelt to say a prayer, and before I could start, I got a prompting, "Don't go to Riverside." It was the exact opposite of what I wanted. I felt disappointed, but knew the Lord wouldn't misguide me. I ended up moving to Stockton, where I met a future business partner. Years later, the business partner and I moved to Hemet, California, near Riverside, where we had the number one business of our kind in the area.

Another time, I had decided to buy a white convertible despite Becky telling me it was a bad investment. Becky's father is a mechanic so she knows about cars. I stubbornly thought, "I'm going to buy it anyway!" The next morning, I woke up and knelt to say a prayer, and immediately got the prompting, "Don't buy the white car." Again, it was the opposite of what I wanted. I felt disappointed, but knew the Lord knew best. Eventually, I got a blue convertible instead, and it was a better car.

Reading Words that Aren't There

Once, I was reading Alma and read something I'd never read before. I went to show Becky, but I couldn't find it. I showed her the page and where it was, but it was no longer there!

Becky read something in her Patriarchal Blessing that she'd never read before. When she tried to show it to me, it was gone!

I think Heavenly Father does this to show that His Word is alive, and not dead. This is why scriptures and words spoken under the influence of the Holy Ghost can be called the *living word* of God.

<u>Revelation</u>

Revelation is learning directly from Divinity. Elder Richard G. Scott gave a talk in General Conference of April 2012, "How to Obtain Revelation for Your Personal Life." He talked about the difference between inspiration and revelation. He said:

> The Holy Ghost communicates important information that we need to guide us in our mortal journey. When it is crisp and clear and essential, it warrants the title of revelation. When it is a series of promptings we often have to guide us step by step to a worthy objective, for the purpose of this message, it is inspiration.

Notice how Elder Scott said that revelation is information from the Holy Ghost that is "essential." In my experience, revelation is based on need as when one is in danger. For example, "And the Lord warned Omer in a dream that he should depart out of the land; wherefore Omer departed out of the land with his family, and traveled many days" (Ether 9:3). This revelation through a dream was prompted by the danger that Omer and his family faced. It was essential to their safety.

Xena Henderson wrote her "People Stories" about people from another planet with spiritual abilities. Some of the people on earth begin to develop spiritual abilities too. When the people with spiritual abilities sense that someone is in trouble, they usually ask, "Is there a need?"

Premonitions

Premonitions are thoughts or feelings that something is going to happen before it does. Have you ever thought about a person you hadn't contacted in a long time, the phone rings, and it's that person? My observation is that people who experience this type of mental connection have an emotional bond; it rarely happens with strangers.

Another explanation for this phenomenon is Carl Jung's idea of Synchronicity. Synchronicity means that something happens at the same time because of a meaningful connection.

Some theorists say premonitions are based on Extra-Sensory Perception, or ESP. Joseph Banks Rhine and Louisa Ella Rhine found evidence for ESP in experiments during the 1930s. Later scientist conducted the same experiments using tighter and tighter controls until the findings went away. They explain some of the early evidence for ESP as coincidence. Some people believe that nothing happens by coincidence.

Does observing a spiritual phenomenon in an experiment actually change it? The famous Double-Slit experiment showed that light acted as a wave until mechanical observation was set up to observe it, then it acted like a particle. The act of observing the light changed the way it behaved. Scientists still do not know why this is so.

The Double-Slit experiment provides a metaphor to how miracles work. "Now faith is the substance of things hoped for, the evidence of things not seen" (Hebrews 11:1). I can pray for a miracle while having faith that it will happen. That is much different than if I pray for a miracle while wishing to observe evidence for it. Having faith that something will happen is much different than wanting evidence, or doubting that it will happen at all. Mark wrote about Jesus going to his hometown of Nazareth, "And he could there do no mighty work, save that he laid his hands upon a few sick folk, and healed them. And he marveled because of their unbelief" (6:5).

Joseph Smith said:

> A person may profit by the first intimation of the spirit of revelation; for instance, when you feel pure intelligence flowing into you, it may give you sudden strokes of ideas, so that by noticing it, you may find it fulfilled the same day or soon; (i.e.) those things that were presented unto your minds by the Spirit of God, will come to pass; and thus by learning the Spirit of God and understanding it, you may grow into the principle of revelation, until you become perfect in Christ Jesus (History of the

Church 3:381).

Gamma Rays in the brain are the fastest and highest brainwaves. They are associated with intelligence, compassion, self-control, happiness, increased awareness of the senses, intuition, spirituality, altruism, transcendence, universal love, and higher virtues. Could this be what Joseph Smith called "pure intelligence flowing into you"?

Spiritual Gifts

Heavenly Father is perfect. He created us as imperfect beings. He gives us weaknesses so that we can choose to be humble (see Ether 12:24). He also gives us talents.

No one is better than anyone else. We are all equal before God. However, some people are better at certain things than others. Someone could be the best basketball player in the world, but not bilingual.

Everyone you meet will be better than you at something and worse than you at something else. Even babies are good at cheering people up even though they can't walk or talk. God wanted us all to be imperfect. That way no one is overall better or worse than anyone else.

Because Heavenly Father gave us each unique talents, we have different spiritual gifts. Paul talked about spiritual gifts in 1 Corinthians 12-10. It is up to us to exercise these gifts and develop them. Heavenly Father is perfect and has all spiritual gifts.

<u>Scriptural Liahona</u>

My brother uses the scriptures as a personal Liahona. (The Liahona is a divine compass in the Book of Mormon.) My brother opens the scriptures to a random verse as inspiration for what is going on in his life at that time. He has been blessed greatly by this.

I have tried to use the scriptures as a personal Liahona. I have had a few successes at this when I have been in the Temple. Otherwise, it doesn't seem to be my spiritual gift.

<u>Predictions in Literature and Music</u>

Books and songs have strangely predicted the future. There are various explanations for this phenomenon. They could be divinely inspired. They could be self-fulfilling prophecies. They could be satanic conspiracies. The human originators may or may not be aware of what is going on.

In 1838, Edgar Allen Poe published a story about a shipwreck in which three sailors ate a fourth, named Richard Parker. Forty-six years later, a real yacht was shipwrecked, and three sailors ate the cabin boy, named Richard Parker.

Fourteen years before the Titanic sank, Walter Lord wrote a book about the Titan sinking. The book is so close to the actual events that people called Mr. Lord Clairvoyant. Mr. Lord denied it, saying he just knew about ships.

Jules Vern predicted advances in exploration by balloon and submarine. He denied being a prophet, saying he took good notes on science articles he'd read.

Jules Vern inspired my favorite science fiction author, Ray Bradbury. Ray Bradbury inspired other science fiction writers, authors of children's books, and even Stephen King.

As a teenager, I read many of Ray Bradbury's short stories. One critic derided "Dandelion Wine" as "dripping with sentimentality." That's why I loved it! As an adult, I read that Ray Bradbury called Jesus Christ a myth. My respect for him fell.

Ray Bradbury's stories predicted headphones, wall-to-wall TV screens, videophones, political correctness, loneliness due to electronics, self-driving cars, electronic surveillance, ATMs, artificial intelligence, and "the butterfly effect."

Three predictions were even more strangely accurate; Fahrenheit 451 portrayed dialysis as a common medical practice, which it has since become. When O.J. Simpson fled from the Police on live television, Russell Baker wrote in his New York Times column that he saw Fahrenheit 451 come to life. Farenheit 451 also predicted interactive television shows, like Netflix's "Black Mirror: Bandersnatch."

Music can also be strangely similar to actual events. The Scorpions' song, "Winds of Change," synchronized with the breakdown of the USSR. Coldplay's song, "Viva la Vida," had many parallels to Saddam

Hussein.

Burning in the Bosom

This is one of the most common descriptions of the Spirit. It comes from Doctrine and Covenants 9:8 in which the Lord tells Oliver Cowdery, "If it is right I will cause that your bosom shall burn within you; therefore, you shall feel it is right." This scripture is personal to Oliver Cowdery. It doesn't mean that everyone feels the Spirit this way.

Remembering Spiritual Experiences

John 14:26 says, "But the Comforter, which is the Holy Ghost, whom the Father will send in my name, he shall teach you all things, and bring all things to your remembrance, whatsoever I have said unto you." The Holy Ghost can remind us of a scripture that applies to a problem we are having. It can also make us forget.

Stupor of Thought

This also comes from Doctrine and Covenants 9:8, "If it be not right you shall have no such feelings, but you shall have a stupor of thought that shall cause you to forget the thing which is wrong."

Receiving an Impression

Sometimes when I give a Priesthood blessing, I get an impression of what to say, but I don't have language to describe the impression. I end up using the closest words I can, but I know they are inadequate to explain the spiritual impression. Joseph Smith said that revelation from God comes to "our spirits precisely as though we had no bodies at all," (See Smith, Joseph Fielding .1989. Teachings of the Prophet Joseph Smith, Deseret Book Company, Salt Lake City, Utah, p. 355).

The language of the Holy Spirit does not use words. Anyone who has attempted to explain spiritual matters to an atheist realizes this inadequacy of spoken language.

In Romans 8:26, Paul talks about the Holy Spirit helping us with our prayers with "groanings which cannot be uttered." Likewise, Paul said he was "caught up into Paradise, and heard unspeakable words" (2 Corinthians 12:4).

In 3 Nephi 17:16–17, the people wrote about Jesus praying with them:

> The eye hath never seen, neither hath the ear heard, before, so great and marvelous things as we saw and heard Jesus speak unto the Father; and no tongue can speak, neither can there be written by any man, neither can the hearts of men conceive so great and marvelous things as we both saw and heard Jesus speak; and no one can conceive of the joy which filled our souls at the time we heard him pray for us unto the Father.

Emphasizing Words in Scripture

The Holy Spirit can emphasize words in scripture

to enhance their meaning. Once, I was reading about the Mount of Transfiguration in Matthew 17:5 and the Spirit emphasized the word, "This," as in "*This* is my beloved son." It made me think that Peter's suggestion to build three tabernacles for Jesus, Moses, and Elijah offended Heavenly Father as it put Jesus on the same level as the other two, so Heavenly Father corrected Peter in a way that left him on the ground, shaking in fear.

Ideas

When I was High Priest Group Leader, I got an idea to change a home teaching assignment. I did so. Some of the home teachers didn't like the change. One of the home teachers took his new assignment seriously. He drove by one of his new homes every day. Once, he saw the door standing open. He went over and called the brother's name. The brother answered and said he couldn't get up. The home teacher rescued him and got him help. The home teacher took care of him for a few months until he passed on. I got the idea to change the home teaching assignments back to the way they were before. I didn't know that that brother was going to need help when he did, but Heavenly Father knew!

Precognition

The mother of one of my clients said her daughter was precognizant. The mother said she was driving one day and stopped at a stop sign. Her daughter jumped out of the car and said, "Someone died here." The daughter refused to go further, saying, "I don't want them to get me." The mother had to take the daughter a different route. The mother thought it was strange. A few days later, the mother drove by the same intersection alone, and there was a memorial set up on the side of the road for someone who had died there.

The same mother said that her daughter refused to go inside the house. She asked why. The daughter said she would fall in a hole. Later, the city came by and condemned that house and four others because they were built over a sinkhole.

Discernment

For every gift of the Holy Spirit, the devil has a counterfeit gift. How do we know what is a holy gift and what is unholy?

Meditation can be good. Joseph F. Smith prayed and meditated before receiving his vision of the spirit world. (See Teachings of the Presidents of the Church, Joseph F. Smith, The Church of Jesus Christ of Latter-day Saints, Salt Lake City, page 362.) Meditation can also be evil.

There are many questionable spiritual experiences, including Astral projection, Clairvoyance, Levitation, Mediumship or Séance, Remote Viewing, Spoon Bending, Telepathy, and Telekinesis.

Scott Adams, Cartoonist and scholar of hypnotism, said he doesn't believe in past lives because people who told him about their past lives only remembered being famous, glamorous, or exotic people from the past, never ordinary people.

Spiritual gifts are signs that "shall follow them that believe" (Mark 16:17). Many spiritual gifts were poured out upon the early Church of Jesus Christ of Latter-day Saints. Likewise, some false spirits deceived early members of the Church in Kirkland, Ohio. (See Manuscript History of the Church, vol. C-1, page 1311, josephsmithpapers.org.)

Spiritual Laws

Spiritual laws are just as real as physical laws, like the Law of Gravity. Maybe they are more real.

I wrote, "Do I Really Believe the Scriptures?", about spiritual laws. I believed the promises in the scriptures figuratively. As my spirituality grew, I decided to test the scriptures *literally.* I found that the promises were very literal.

I read about a couple complaining to a Jewish therapist that they were tired and worn out all the time. The Jewish therapist told them to observe a day of rest. They said, "But we're atheists." The Jewish therapist told them that the day of rest would work for them anyway. They tried it, and it helped them feel much more awake and energetic. Of course, they didn't receive other blessings of the Sabbath, but the spiritual laws of God work when we obey them, even if we don't believe in them. When people wondered who taught Jesus, he told them, "My doctrine is not mine, but his that sent me. If any man will do his will, he shall know of the doctrine, whether it be of God, or whether I speak of myself" (John 7:16–17). Jesus revealed through Joseph Smith, "There is a law irrevocably decreed in heaven before the foundations of the world, upon which all blessings are predicated— And when we obtain any blessing from God, it is by obedience to that law upon which it is predicated" (Doctrine and Covenants 130:20–21).

God follows divine laws. Alma the Younger told his son, Corianton, that God had to follow the law of justice, "if not so, the works of justice would be destroyed, and God would cease to be God. But God ceaseth not to be God" (Alma 42:22–23). Joseph Smith said the following:

> God himself, finding he was in the midst of spirits and glory, because he was more intelligent, saw proper to institute laws whereby the rest could have a privilege to advance like himself. The relationship we have with God places us in a situation to advance in knowledge. He has power to institute laws to instruct the weaker intelligences, that they may be exalted with himself, so that they might have one glory upon another, and all that knowledge, power, glory, and intelligence, which is requisite in order to save them" (Teachings of the Prophet Joseph Smith by Joseph Fielding Smith, p. 354).

Another spiritual law is if you give, you will receive a hundred fold. This has been confirmed literally several times in my life. I was so excited about this law because I thought I would be independently wealthy in a short amount of time. I wondered why it didn't happen.

I was driving to the store to buy boxes for an upcoming move from California to Utah. I passed a boy with a sign, asking for money for a funeral. I felt a prompting to give the twenty-dollar bill I had in my pocket. I rationalized that I needed money now more than ever. Later that day, I found that my vehicle needed a two-hundred dollar repair. It wasn't a coincidence.

I learned that the opposite of the spiritual Law of Giving is true as well. If I refuse to give when able, I lose a hundred fold. Just as the Law of Giving is literal, so is the Law of Not Giving!

The Power of Words

Dr. Masaru Emoto studied how words changed the shape of water molecules. Positive words brought order, symmetry, and beauty. Negative words brought chaos, array, and tension. Because our bodies are about sixty percent water, Dr. Emoto concluded that words affect our bodies in much the same way. He recorded his findings in his book, "The Hidden Messages in Water."

Skeptics dismissed Dr. Emoto's studies as pseudoscience. However, many people have recreated his experiments in other ways. One experiment is to cut an apple in half, put both halves in jars, speak positive words to one half and negative words to another half. Videos show that one half will stay fresh longer while the other will begin to spoil quicker. Experiments show similar effects on plants, rice, and other things.

I tested the power of words out on a bamboo plant that a coworker gave to me. I told it to live, thrive, and grow. I blessed it. After three days, it broke the glass jar it was in!

These experiments are wonderfully simple to reproduce. Even skeptics can do so!

Rational Explanation

A friend and I were talking about spiritual phenomena. I said, "There's always a rational explanation." He thought I was denying that spiritual phenomena existed. I said I believed that the spiritual phenomena were true, but that people could always find non-spiritual explanations for them, and that's why they don't believe in spirituality. He agreed.

People who don't believe in spirituality do a disservice to themselves. They deny what is going on all around them. When they experience miracles, they explain them ways that make sense to their rational minds. This doesn't discount the reality of the miracles. People who deny spirituality have to find other explanations for faith, religion, and miracles. They expect these things to end when they are actually increasing, and will keep increasing until they fill the world. When God sends fire from Heaven for a specific cause, they will say it was nature and chance.

Skepticism is healthy if kept in balance. Too little skepticism leads to gullibility; too much leads to cynicism. Even scientists must make tiny leaps of faith to formulate hypotheses, even if those hypotheses were suggested by other studies.

Science

Human science is limited. We can't even cure the common cold. Conversely, God is omniscient. Aeronautics says it is impossible for a bumblebee to fly. Divine science says otherwise.

Rupert Sheldrake gave a TED Talk called, "The Science Delusion." He said that scientists had difficulty working with time and gravity because they all had slightly different calculations about time and gravity. To correct for these differences, Western scientists averaged many calculations and established them as *constant* values for time and gravity. They have been treating time and gravity as constants ever since. The only problem is they are not constants. They are *variables.* Scientists can establish rules for convenience, but the cost is in truth.

Scientists criticize many studies on spirituality, and their criticisms are sound, yet they do not offer any alternative studies. When you only have imperfect studies to go on, you must go on them until you have less imperfect studies. For example, vaccines were considered safe after one study tested one type of vaccine. The results were generalized to all vaccines. This is bad science by any definition. It's like proving a medicine cured one disease then claiming it cures all diseases. Of course, that's been done too.

Marijuana supporters are like old Western snake oil peddlers. "Whatever your ill," they cry, "Marijuana will cure it!" I don't argue that Marijuana can't alleviate symptoms, but the claim that it can cure every disease is—forgive the pun—smoke!

My wife's brother smoked Marijuana to alleviate his pain from Leukemia. He also became angry to his family. My wife's last days with him were unpleasant. My wife's sister smokes Marijuana for her diseases, and acts like a jerk. I don't claim that all who smoke Marijuana are angry jerks; I just say that it has negative effects as well as positive.

The same things that are said about Marijuana today were said about Cocaine in the past.

Science follows an "inch-worming" method where each study builds on a previous study to expand our knowledge inch by inch. Such a model requires no great leaps of faith. However, I read in college that Albert Einstein said he would think about an idea for a long time as if he were banging his head against a wall then when he purposely took a break and did nothing, the answer would suddenly and intuitively come into his mind. (I've tried to find the reference many times since, but there are so many Einstein quotes that it is like trying to find a needle in a haystack.)

Einstein's description reminds me of Joseph Smith's quote, "A person may profit by the first intimation of the spirit of revelation; for instance, when you feel pure intelligence flowing into you, it may give you sudden strokes of ideas" (History of the Church 3:381). Could they be describing the same experience?

Materialists deny the existence of God, the Holy Spirit, and human spirits. Science is completely compatible with God; however, Materialists argue that they are incompatible.

Materialists denounce any investigation into spiritual matters as pseudoscience. They discourage scientific inquiry into spiritual matters, saying that it is a dead end. Why are they so reluctant to study spiritual matters?

Mental Health Treatment

I went to two trainings with Dr. Mark Ragins, director of the Village, an experimental voluntary mental health treatment program in Los Angeles. He would talk to patients about their symptoms and asked if they tried a certain medication. If they said they hadn't, he would ask them if they wanted to try it. He also offered them jobs around the village, but if they didn't show up or do a quality job, they would get fired.

During training, Dr. Ragins said that the first mental health treatment programs in the United States of America were run by the Quakers. Their treatment model was simple; mental illness meant that you had lost your way with God. If you found your way, you would get better. They had a ninety percent recovery rate. He asked us what the recovery rates in our agencies were. If the agency where I worked at the time had thirty to forty percent recovery rate, we thought it was good!

Miracles

When something has been shown to be scientifically valid, Materialists argue that there is some mechanism besides God that explains it. Healings are explained as some power of nature that we cannot understand. This is the very definition of miracle as given by Orson Pratt, who said that miracles followed natural laws that humans don't fully comprehend. Speaking about the flood, he said:

> It may be enquired, what natural laws could have performed such an event? I do not pretend to say that any regular, uniform laws exist by which it was accomplished; but there are laws, perhaps, that finite man does not comprehend and fully understand, which might occasion the division of the earth. The Lord has under his control all the laws of nature, whether uniform or

not. It is just as easy for the Lord to cause water to stand up as perpendicular walls, instanced in the case of the children of Israel crossing the Red Sea, as it is to cause these waters to settle to their common level. What causes water to find its level? It is the power of God, and nothing else. We give it the name of gravitation; but the power of gravitation is nothing more nor less than the power God exercises upon the elements, producing uniform laws (Journal of Discourses, Vol. 18, p. 317, http://jod.mrm.org/18).

Prayer

Studies have shown that prayers can help people heal quicker. See Harris, W.S.; Gowda, M.; Kolb, J.W.; Strychacz, C.P.; Vacek, J.L.; Jones, P.G.; Forker, A.; O'Keefe, J.H.; McCallister, B.D. (1999). "A randomized, controlled trial of the effects of remote, intercessory prayer on outcomes in patients admitted to the coronary care unit". Arch Intern Med. 159 (19): 2273–78. See also Leibovici, L (2001). "Effects of remote, retroactive intercessory prayer on outcomes in patients with bloodstream infection: randomized controlled trail". BMJ. 323 (7327): 1450–51.

Materialists denounce studies on prayer as unscientific. Even if there is an observable mechanism at work, they argue, it could be the power of humans themselves, but not of God.

One of my clients had a neighbor who played his

radio loudly, late at night. She asked him to turn it down several times, but he refused. Not knowing what else to do, she prayed for help. The neighbor moved out and a nun moved in. The nun lived a quiet life.

Angels

Angels are beautiful spirits with power and glory. One of my friends from work saw a beautiful angel with the most muscular and healthy-looking face he'd ever seen.

The most common, immediate human reaction at seeing an angel is fear. This is why angels so often say, "fear not" (See Matthew 28:5, Luke 1:13, Luke 1:30, Luke 2:10, and Acts 27:24). When Joan of Arc first saw Saint Michael, Saint Margaret, and Saint Catherine, she was afraid, but after her initial fear left, she felt comfort and peace. When Joseph Smith saw the Angel Moroni, he said, "When I first looked upon him, I was afraid; but the fear soon left me" (Joseph Smith History 1:32).

Babies stare at the ceiling or at blank space, and make noises, laugh, and reach out as if they were interacting with a person. Many young children have "invisible friends," with whom they talk and interact.

Death

Materialists believe in Annihilation, that death is "eternal oblivion." Alma desired something similar just before he was converted. He said, "Oh, thought I, that I could be banished and become extinct both soul and body, that I might not be brought to stand in the presence of my god, to be judged of my deeds" (Alma 36:15). Maybe annihilation is the natural desire of someone separated from God when thinking about coming back into God's presence.

Life After Death

Robert Blatchford was an atheist who wrote books attacking religion. When his wife died, he told a friend, "It is she, and yet it is not she. Everything is changed. Something that was there before is taken away. She is not the same. What can be gone if it be not the soul?" (More Things in Heaven and Earth: Adventures in Quest of a Soul, 1925).

Dr. Jon Connelly, founder of Rapid Resolution Therapy, was quoted by Kristin Rivas, saying, "Who you are cannot be defined by your body. I know you have a foot, but that you are not your foot. If something happened to your foot, I wouldn't say, "Hey Kristin, I'm glad most of you made it here today." He continued with the following:

I don't know all the answers about what happens after we die, but I do know that science says we are all made of energy, and energy can neither be created nor destroyed. I know that our five senses fool us sometimes, and we have to take things on faith like a child asking his parents,

"Where did the sun go?" on a cloudy and a rainy day. (See The Life-Changing Power of Words: Kristin Rivas at TEDxRainier.)

Duncan MacDougall (1866-1920) hypothesized that the weight of a human soul was 21 grams, and conducted experiments about it. Materialists have declared his experiments unscientific.

<u>Peace After a Loved One Dies</u>

When clients come to me for grief/loss therapy, I show them a scene from Patch Adams (1998). In the scene, Dr. Adams, played by Robin Williams, loses his head nurse. He's angry and depressed. He goes to her favorite spot and confronts God. Then, he sees a butterfly like the ones the nurse used to watch. It helps him find peace after her death.

Sometimes, I think we put our own thoughts and feelings onto a deceased loved one. We have difficulty accepting our loved one dying so we assume our loved one had difficulty accepting it.

When I lived in Stockton, California, I heard about a ten or eleven-year-old boy who was caught in crossfire. Several of my clients had loved ones caught in crossfire. It was more than a rare occurrence there. This boy was hit in the spinal cord and paralyzed from the waist down. People felt terrible for him, saying things like, "He'll never run again!" Conversely, the boy said he was just glad to be alive. He wheeled himself around in a wheelchair, shooting basketball. Those people were putting their feelings onto the boy. He obviously felt differently about his situation.

One of my Native American clients had a dream about horses after his father. Because in his tradition, horses represented deceased loved ones, the dream brought him peace.

Presence of a Deceased Loved One

A study of two hundred and ninety-three widows in England found that almost half of them reported feeling the presence of their deceased spouses. A smaller percentage, saw, heard, or felt their spouses (Rees, 1971). Feeling the presence of a deceased spouse is a common human experience according to this study. (See Rees, W.D. 1971. The hallucinations of widowhood. British Medical Journal, 4, 37–41.) When almost half of subjects experience something, it is not an anomaly, it is a common human experience.

One of my clients said she was driving in her car, thinking about how much she missed her mother, who had passed away about a year earlier. Suddenly, she smelled her mother's perfume and felt as if her mother was sitting next to her in the passenger seat. It comforted her that death was not the end of existence.

I have felt my late mother's presence at important times in my life, including my wedding and the births of my children. My grandfather told me that he felt the presence of my grandmother every day after she died. My uncle did not believe in life after death. As he prepared for death, I told him about my experiences and what my grandfather told me. He said it was all in our minds, a form of "wish fulfillment." I believe he knows differently now that he has passed on!

The Other Side

One of my clients said his grandmother liked to sit in a rocking chair by the fireplace. She usually sat and played with the children, but she also turned toward the mantle where she had pictures of family members who had passed on. Over time, she played with the children less and less, and looked at the pictures more and more. He said it was as if she were preparing to cross over to "the other side."

Terminal Lucidity

Terminal Lucidity is when someone has a moment of clarity right before they die. It is more significant when people are in a coma and they suddenly come awake, or if they have Alzheimer's, and they are suddenly themselves again. Ronald Reagan had a moment like this before he died. Terminal Lucidity can be a blessing to family members who take the opportunity to make peace and say goodbye to their loved ones.

Deathbed Visions

Many people who are dying report seeing family members coming to meet them when they die and to ease their passing. Death does not seem to hold much sting in situations like this.

<u>Memorial Service</u>

When I was a young adult, a good friend of mine died. His family asked if I would speak at the memorial service. I agreed. I was disappointed that the family had buried my friend in a private ceremony. I thought the memorial service would not be as meaningful after the burial.

The family had a large, framed picture of my friend, smiling. I felt my friend's presence at the memorial service. I realized there was no difference between a funeral and a memorial service. In fact, I might like the memorial service even better!

Near Death Experiences

Near Death Experiences (NDEs) have been rejected by mainstream scientists, who give various alternative explanations. These alternative explanations seem more plausible to those who have not had NDEs; however, they fail to convince any that have had NDEs.

NDEs are similar across time. A circa 1510 painting by Hieronymous Bosch, Ascent of the Blessed, shows a tunnel of light, which is a common feature of modern NDEs.

NDEs are similar across cultures. Survivors in Christian cultures describe going to Heaven while survivors in Buddhist cultures describe going to Nirvana (Hold, J.M., Grayson, B. & James, D., 2009). (See Holden, Janice Miner; Greyson, Bruce; James, Debbie, eds. 2009. The handbook of near-death experiences thirty years of investigation. Westport, Conn.: Praeger Publishers.)

Lehi from the Book of Mormon saw a "pillar of fire" on a rock (1 Nephi 1:6). He described being "carried away in a vision," in which he saw the heavens, God, and numberless angels (1 Nephi 1:8). This is similar to modern NDEs in which people see Heaven.

Later, Lehi had a vision of "a dark and dreary wilderness" (1 Nephi 8:4). He traveled for "many hours in darkness" (1 Nephi 8:7) before asking the Lord for help. This is similar to modern NDEs in which a person is in darkness until calling on the Lord for help.

Joseph Smith's First Vision has similar features to NDEs. He felt a "being from the unseen world" with power and "astonishing influence" attempting to destroy him, and almost succeeding (Joseph Smith History 1:15). Note that Joseph was likely near death at this moment. Then, he "saw a pillar of light" descending to him (Joseph Smith History 1:16). This is similar to a tunnel of light described by so many people who have had NDEs.

People who have experienced NDEs say that they felt a connection with others and everything around them.

NDEs include remote viewing or seeing things from a third-person point of view. Many people with NDEs see their own body and are even surprised by this experience. Some view the room from a point near the ceiling, as if they are floating in the air.

NDEs happen when a person is completely brain dead. Science says it is impossible to think while brain dead. This evidence supports the theory that human thought is not limited to the body, including the brain. Some people call this the mind. Others call it the spirit.

NDEs are different than dreams. People who have had NDEs have talked about things they have heard and seen, and their experiences have been confirmed. One of Dr. Pim Van Lommel's patients, who was in a coma for two weeks, said he saw Dr. Van Lommel remove his dentures and put them in the drawer of a medical cart. Dr. Van Lommel confirmed what the patient saw while in a coma. (See Van Lommel, Pim 2013. Non-local Consciousness: A Concept Based on Scientific Research on Near-Death Experiences During Cardiac Arrest. Journal of Consciousness Studies, Jan-Feb 2013, 1-2, p7- p48, 42)

Memories of NDEs are stored in the same place of the brain as experiences. They are not stored in the same place of the brain as memories of imagined events. (See Palmieri, Arianna; Vincenzo Calvo, Johann R. Kleinbub, Federica Meconi, Matteo Marangoni, Paolo Barilaro, Alice Broggio, Marco Sambin, and Paola Sessa. 2014. "Reality" of near-death-experience memories: Evidence from a psychodynamic and electrophysiological integrated study. Frontiers in Human Neuroscience, Vol 8, Jun 19, 2014. ArtID: 429.)

NDEs are different than using medications or drugs, as explained by people who have experienced both.

Dr. Eben Alexander was a neurologist and an atheist. He did not believe in spirits or life after death. He said that NDEs were hallucinations. Then, he had a serious brain disease that left him in a coma for a week. The disease should have killed him, but miraculously, he survived. He said an angel took him to Heaven, and God spoke to him about creating the Universe. As a neurologist, he says there is no psychological or physiological explanation for his NDE; the only explanation is spiritual. (See Alexander, Eben. 2012. Proof of Heaven: A Neurosurgeon's Journey into the Afterlife. Simon and Schuster)

Many other atheists have been converted to a belief in God through NDEs, including Howard Storm.

Many celebrities have had NDEs, including Chad Michael Murray, Liam Hemsworth, Zac Efron, Amy Schumer, Leonardo DiCaprio, Tracy Morgan, Lamar Odom, Amy Purdy, Gerard Butler, Travis Barker, Eminem, Sharon Stone, Morgan Freeman, Jim Caviezel, 50 Cent, William Petersen, Jane Seymour, Peter Sellers, Elizabeth Taylor, Robert Pastorelli, Gary Busey, Larry Hagman, Tony Bennett, Donald Sutherland, Erik Estrada, Burt Reynolds, Chevy Chase, Eric Roberts, George Lucas, Ozzy Osbourne, Nikki Sixx, Roy Horn, Jeremy Kagan, Ronald Reagan, Johnny Cash, George Foreman, and Elvis Presley.

NDEs are different than hallucinations. Hallucinations affect one sense. NDEs involve all the senses, which are heightened beyond normal.

People with NDEs miraculously experience no

permanent brain damage, though their brains have a lack of oxygen for long periods of time.

People have had shared NDEs, where they saw and heard the same things, and carried on entire conversations with each other while unconscious. When they became conscious again, they each remembered their conversation independent of the other person.

Many people say their senses are heightened during NDEs. They see bright and vivid colors. They hear beautiful, ambient music. They smell sweet, floral fragrances. They taste delicious foods. They feel no pain, only security, well-being, and love.

People often feel pain when returning to their bodies after NDEs. They see the world as limited and dreary. They feel sorrow at being confined to the world. They lose their fear of death. They find new purpose in their lives, which is usually to help others.

I have had many clients tell me about their NDEs. They say they can't normally talk about them because people won't understand them or will think they are crazy.

One of my clients said she died in the hospital. She saw "the veil." She looked far to the right and saw someone pass through this veil without the veil moving. She intuitively knew if she passed through it, she wouldn't come back. She saw three spirits around her. They were beautiful and full of light. She decided to go back into her body. When she became conscious, there were three nurses around her bed. One was stroking her hair and crying, and said, "We thought we'd lost you."

Joseph Smith's First Vision has similar features to an NDE. He felt a "being from the unseen world" with power and "astonishing influence" attempting to destroy him, and almost succeeding (Joseph Smith History 1:15). Joseph could have been near death at this moment. Then, he "saw a pillar of light" descending to him (Joseph Smith History 1:16). This is similar to a tunnel of light described by so many people who have had NDEs.

Lehi from the Book of Mormon saw a "pillar of fire" on a rock (1 Nephi 1:6). He described being "carried away in a vision," in which he saw the heavens, God, and numberless angels (1 Nephi 1:8). This is similar to modern NDEs in which people see Heaven.

Later, Lehi had a vision of "a dark and dreary wilderness" (1 Nephi 8:4). He traveled for "many hours in darkness" (1 Nephi 8:7) then "I began to pray unto the Lord that he would have mercy on me, according to the multitude of his tender mercies" (1 Nephi 8:8). This is similar to modern NDEs in which a person is in darkness until calling on the Lord for help.

Divine Protection

One of my clients married a member of the Greek Mafia in California, USA. They had two sons. Her husband began teaching her sons about organized crime. She didn't want them to live that lifestyle. She divorced her husband. He manipulated the Courts and convinced them that she was crazy. He was granted full custody of their two sons. She lost her parental rights. He attempted to kill her several times, but each time she was protected by miraculous means. He gave up, saying that God didn't want her dead. Even though, she had gone into hiding, changed her name, changed her appearance, and changed her telephone number, he continued to harass her. Once, she came out of a store, and he called her new telephone number. He told her the street she was on and what she was wearing. He had eyes everywhere.

My client saw the San Diego Temple. She walked onto the grounds and was greeted by two Sister Missionaries. She said, "God tells me that this is His Church. I want to join." After they recovered from their shock, they taught and eventually baptized her.

My client told me that she used to have a beautiful, ruby necklace worth about seventy-thousand dollars. She realized that the necklace was evil because it distracted her from her true purpose of protecting her sons. She sold it.

Visions

Our culture tends to be skeptical of spiritual dreams and visions. Other cultures view them as an important part of life.

A Native American client told me that she had a dream about a relative who looked black. She later found out that the same day she had the dream, her relative had overdosed on Heroin, had a heart attack, died, and fallen forward, and that his blood had pooled to the front of his body and turned black.

A Cherokee client told me that he saw a vision of a medicine man hundreds of miles away. Later, a car drove up and the same medicine man got out. My client walked up and said the medicine man's name even though they had never met. The medicine man also said my client's name. The medicine man said many things to my client, including that he would live to be a hundred and fourteen years old.

Later, my client said he saw a vision of himself with his future wife and son in California. He moved to California, found his wife, married her, and they had a son.

Native American Spirituality

Once, I talked with a traditional Christian friend about Native American spirituality. My friend said it was all of the devil. I was surprised, but realized I had respect for Native American spirituality because I knew about Christianity among early Native Americans in the Book of Mormon. My friend didn't know about it. I told my friend about crosses on ruins in Central America, Native American legends of a white god who promised to return, and the Native Americans initially believing that the Conquistador Cortes was the legendary god.

On my mission, a Mexican-American family

"adopted" me. The father taught Sunday School. He asked how a handful of Conquistadors could defeat an entire army of their ancestors. He said it wasn't the guns, armor, or horses. It was the belief in the legendary god who could not be killed.

I have a friend who is a member of the Church of Jesus Christ of Latter-day Saints and a Tarahumara of Northern Mexico. His family has had several prophetic visions about the destruction of America. He was surprised that many members of the Church don't have visions. I told him that it was a spiritual gift of Manasseh, the Israelite Tribe of many Native Americans. He asked me, "What was the spiritual gift of Ephraim?", an Israelite Tribe of many Church members.

I said, "Obedience."

Lucid Dreams

The Holy Spirit told a good friend of mine to move from California. He had a dream in which he saw a house with a specific mountain range in the distance. Soon afterwards, he got in his car and drove east. He looked for the mountain range, hoping to find it in Nevada. When he came to the Utah border, he groaned. He didn't want to move to Utah. He decided to visit his mother who lived in a tiny town. He drove to her house. They had a good visit. He decided to look at houses for sale. He called a realtor. The realtor had to drive from a larger town. The realtor drove him around to a few houses in the area. He didn't like them. By inspiration, he asked the realtor to drive down a certain road.

"Turn here," he said.

"We don't have anything that way."

"Turn here anyway." The realtor did. There was an old house with weeds growing all around it. "Stop here," said my friend. They got out. My friend found a "For Sale" sign hidden by weeds. The realtor looked in his information. He couldn't find the house. He called the office. They confirmed that it was for sale, but it was so old, it wasn't on their list. My friend looked up and saw the mountain range from his dream. He bought the house.

Saved from Suicide

Some Buddhists view life as sacred to the point they don't knowingly kill flies. "What right do we have to take any life," they argue, "When we can't give it back?" They have a good point. This kind of reverence for life could go a long way in helping people contemplating suicide.

When I was a teenager, I suddenly had an idea to call a friend. My friend and I saw each other almost every day, but we usually didn't talk on the phone. My friend's brother answered and gave the phone to my friend. I asked my friend how he was doing. He said, "Not good." I asked what was wrong. He said he didn't want to talk about it, but was glad I called. Years later, he confided in me that he had locked himself in a room with a loaded gun to kill himself. My phone call came at that moment.

One of my clients decided to commit suicide. He put a rope in his trunk. He drove toward a secluded place so his family wouldn't find his body. It was around four o'clock in the morning. On the way to the place, a driver pulled up next to him and motioned for him to unroll the window. He did. The driver yelled, "God told me to tell you not to do it!" The drive left.

My client thought, "Either 1) that driver was driving around saying that to everyone, 2) he was crazy, or 3) God really did tell him to tell me that." My client decided that the third explanation was the most likely, so he drove home.

I've had several clients attempt to shoot themselves, but the guns did not fire. One put the gun in his mouth and pulled the trigger. Nothing happened. He went outside and shot at the ground. The gun worked perfectly. He was so shaken that he called a friend and told the friend to sell his gun or find a place to store it until he was no longer depressed.

One of my clients who did shoot himself, put the gun under his chin and pulled the trigger. The bullet scarred his cheek, blinded him in one eye, and blew a hole through his brain and skull. Miraculously, he survived. He got reconstructive face surgery. He had an indentation in his head, which he was going to get fixed eventually. He believed God gave him a second chance at life. He still got depressed, but not to the level of wanting to kill himself.

I've had family members and clients who should

have died in car accidents, but didn't. Some were attempts at suicide. Some were not.

One of my clients jumped out of a moving car, hoping to kill himself. He suffered a severe Traumatic Brain Injury. He was sensitive to light and noise. He had major short and long-term memory problems. He had seizures. He couldn't control his emotions, crying at jokes and laughing when he was sad. He said that although he had much more reason to kill himself after his accident, it ironically gave him the desire to live.

One of my clients attempted suicide eleven times by different methods. He tried shooting himself in the head and the heart. He attempted to stab himself. He attempted to slit his wrist and neck. He attempted to electrocute himself in a bathtub. He attempted to drown himself, and more. Each time, something would go wrong with his plans. The last time I saw him, his arm and leg were in casts, and he walked with a crutch. He said he drove off a cliff, his car was totaled, and he was bruised and battered, but he survived. I asked if he thought he would attempt again. He said he wasn't going to attempt again because it wouldn't work anyway. He believed God wanted him alive.

A sex offender said he had mood swings for as long as he could remember. He took a sharp, buck knife to his wrist and was about to slash it open, a friend called and said, "I got the feeling I should call you." The sex offender served seven years in prison. Afterwards, he got flooded with depression, anxiety, and anger. He decided to drive off the road. He drove his truck toward a curve. Right before he got there, his emotions went away, and he felt completely calm for the first time in his life. He heard a voice say, "Don't do it." He turned his truck just in time. He hit the curb with his side wheels, but stayed on the road.

A man died of natural causes, but was resuscitated. Later, he decided to kill himself. He stole his father-in-law's gun and one bullet. He said goodbye to his friends. He drove toward a remote location he had selected. On the way, he was pulled over and arrested. It saved his life. He hung himself in prison, but was resuscitated. After he got out of prison, he took thirty Xanax, got drunk, and put a hose in his car window. His car ran out of gas. He woke up freezing.

All of my clients who miraculously survived suicide had been abused as children. It would make sense that God did not want them to kill themselves because of problems which were not their faults. Of course, I have had former clients who succeeded in committing suicide. I don't know why some were saved and others were not. God knows.

Evil Spirits

A couple came to see me because they were having terrible experiences with "ghosts." The woman said the ghosts pushed her off the bed. Her husband tried to help her, but he was thrown against the wall. I completed my assessment and set up an appointment for them with the psychiatrist as per my usual practice.

In my own experience, I learned that evil spirits could manipulate the physical world. I didn't know to what extent. The couple's experience bothered me, so I asked trusted friends if spirits could throw people against the wall. One said, "If you put yourself in the power of the devil, he can do dangerous things." Another said that when he was on a mission, he became sick and lay down in bed, and the devil physically picked him up off his bed and dropped him onto the floor.

About a month later, the couple who had problems with ghosts came back. The psychiatrist had given them psychotropic medications, and the ghosts had completely gone away.

An eighteen-year-old male told me, "When I was four years old in Mexico, I opened a little door under the stairs and saw a little girl." He said the girl became his best friend and worst enemy. He said, "She told me I am not worth anything, no one will ever love me." The girl told him to "destroy something, throw rocks at cars." He said, "I have full blown conversations with her, points of life, and she answers, and I've learned a lot of things. The most important thing I have learned on life; everyone has to work to make it, nothing is equal. She will tell me that we have to do something about that. She taught me that life is messed up, out of whack. I can't argue with that. She is like a philosopher in my head." Having philosophical discussions doesn't sound so bad, but then he talked about another part of the girl. He said, "The nasty part comes out at night. She is like the angel of my nightmare. I would feel the bed shake. I would pray and it would stop, but it does not work anymore." Later, he said, "The bed does not shake anymore now that I hear the voice more clearly." He said, "The worst thing she told me was to set people on fire. The nasty part of her comes out at school to hurt everyone. They would piss me off." One way to explain this is that the man would get confused or angry and the girl was a psychological extension of his own emotions. Another way to explain it was that the girl was drawn to his emotions of confusion and anger.

Mental Illness and Possession

Matthew wrote about Jesus, "And his fame went throughout all Syria: and they brought unto him all sick people that were taken with divers diseases and torments, and those which were possessed with devils, and those which were lunatic, and those that had the palsy; and he healed them" (4:24).

King James' religious scholars used "lunatic" to mean mentally ill because they believed mental illness was caused by the moon. Matthew writes "those which were possessed with devils, and those which were lunatic," as two different problems. This could mean that being possessed and being mentally ill are two distinct experiences.

M. Scott Peck (1936–2005) was a famous psychiatrist and the author of "The Road Less Traveled." He also wrote about the existence of evil in, "People of the Lie." He wrote that he didn't believe mental illness was caused by the devil, but mental illness could result from resistance to diabolical influences. He also expected demonic possession to be listed among mental illnesses in his lifetime.

Howard Pittman, a Baptist Minister, had a near-death experience in which he viewed demons mimicking mental illnesses. In other words, some people have real mental illnesses and some people have demonic influence that pretend to be mental illnesses.

Psychoses

Psychoses are breaks with reality, including visual hallucinations, auditory hallucinations, and delusional thinking. It is more common than most people think. A review of studies found that the percentage of people who experience hallucinations is between fifteen and twenty-five. (See Irwin, H.J. 1985. Flight of Mind: a psychological study of the out-of-body experience. Metuchen, New Jersey: The Scarecrow Press.) Studies show that most people with Dementia of the Alzheimer's Type experience psychoses during the course of their illness. (See Finkel SI. Behavioral and psychological symptoms of dementia: a current focus for clinicians, researchers, and caregivers. Also see J Clin Psychiatry. 2001. 62 Suppl 21. 3-6. And Hassett A. Psychotic disorder in older persons. Curr Opin Psychiatry. 2001;14:37-381.) Such numbers show that psychoses are not abnormal human experiences, but normal human reaction to stress.

Sleep

Gilgamesh, the oldest non-Biblical book in the world, said, "He who conquers death must first conquer sleep." Another way of putting it is how can you live forever if you can't even stay awake for very long? God never sleeps. He never rests. If you think you are tough, try squatting in place for five minutes! I've done it. It's not easy. God can do that and never get tired.

Buddhists recognize the time just before sleep as a bridge to the spiritual world. Hypnagogic experiences happen when you are falling asleep. Have you ever been in the process of falling asleep, heard the phone ring or a knock at the door, and answered, but no one was there? Some people count this as dreaming, but studies show that it is a different brain pattern than dreaming.

Sleep Paralysis happens when you wake up. Have you ever woken up and couldn't move? Did you feel like something was holding you down or sitting on your chest? Were you unable to call out or make a noise? Did you feel fear? This is a common human experience. Many scientific explanations have been proposed and seem to be sound rational explanations for this phenomena, but rational explanations aren't always true explanations.

Extreme hunger and Thirst

Extreme hunger and thirst can lead to psychoses. Someone told me that Navy Seals are trained to go without food, water, or sleep. Toward the end of training, the trainees tend to lose all sense of time. Their trainers try to trick them into believing they have a long time to go, as if trying to make them give up just before they pass the test.

Sensory Deprivation

Sensory Deprivation for long periods of time result in psychoses in almost every subject. Some began to experience psychoses right away. (See Mason, O; Brady, F (2009). "The psychotomimetic effects of short-term sensory deprivation". Journal of Nervous and Mental Disease 197 (10): 783–785.)

Loneliness

In Castaway (2000), Tom Hanks plays a man who crashed on a deserted island. He draws a face on a volleyball and begins talking to it. Some might argue that he didn't really believe the ball was alive, but he grows attached to the ball and is traumatized when he loses it.

Substances

LSD is known for causing psychoses. However, alcohol causes hallucinations in some people. So can Marijuana and Meth. When my father-in-law gave up cigarettes after years of smoking, he experienced visual hallucinations.

Ideas of Reference

Ideas of reference are delusions in which people think arbitrary things apply to them literally or symbolically. For instance, some people think the television or radio is talking to them personally. One of my clients in the crisis residential home said when he heard a siren he used to think it was a sign that he would be arrested later that week. His peer responded that when he hears a siren, it's a sign that he's about to be arrested! Another client was worried that his wife would find out about his affair. He saw a woman throwing a rug over the railing on her balcony. He thought it was a sign to him that his affair would be covered.

Positive Psychoses

Many people that experience psychoses view them as negative; however, some view them as neutral. A small number view them as positive.

I worked in a crisis residential home in California. One of my clients was a Shaman from Thailand. She spoke with spirits. A Social Worker came to the home to speak with her. Fortunately, we had a staff member who could interpret. The Social Worker attempted to convince my client that she had a mental illness and that the voices she heard were hallucinations. My client told the Social Worker that she was not mentally ill, but she had a spiritual gift. The Social Worker argued with my client for about twenty minutes. Finally, my client stood up and walked away.

I had another client who told me that whenever he spent time with his family or did something nice for someone, he heard voices commending him, but whenever he did something selfish or mean, the voices would tell him to stop.

Opposition to Religion

Sometimes, psychoses happen in opposition to religion, causing chaos around religious events or attempting to punish people going to church. This makes sense if it is the work of evil spirits.

A client told me that when his girlfriend used Meth, she would read the Bible loudly and quickly. He said she was not religious, and only read the Bible when she was using Meth. Other Meth users have told me similar stories.

A client with schizophrenia told me that her voices would "go crazy" whenever she went to church. Even if she drove past a church, they would get louder and begin yelling at her.

A teen client of mine told me she liked The Exorcist and "those kinds of movies." She said shadow people spoke to her. Her aunt gave her a Bible. She said it burned her.

Another teen said she watched horror movies. She heard a voice that told her to kill her mother. When she went to church, she felt like she was being strangled.

A mother told me that her adult son, who had schizophrenia, took a crucifix off the wall, twisted the figure of Jesus Christ off of it, and attempted to stab her with the feet.

Possession

I treated a twelve-year-old male with an intellectual disability. He said that when he got angry, "the other me" came from "the dark" and said, "Let me take over." He said, "No." A school peer punched him, causing him to drop his lunch tray. He managed his anger and got another tray. Four male peers came to "jump" him. He said "the other me" took over then later "went out" of his body. He couldn't remember what had happened. He noticed blood on his arms. He thought, "What did I do? I think it was the other me that did this. He's the one to blame." He said he looked into the mirror, and, "I saw the other me talking to me," "my eyes were black and weird," and, "the other me said he would come back when I was really angry." He said "the other me went into an egg," when he got angry, the egg would crack, and the "other me" would come out. He said that when he got angry, it was the imagination of the other me, and the other me was saying bad words and cussing.

One of my colleagues was a member of the restored Church. He worked as Lead Clinician in a crisis residential home. He told me that a female Clinician and he were interviewing a new client. The client looked at the female Clinician and said, "You Presbyterians are alright." He then looked at my colleague and said, "But not you

Mormons!" After the client left, the female Clinician asked my colleague, "How did he know our religions?"

Once, my colleague and I intervened during a fight. My colleague separated the two residents who were fighting. He told me to sit next to a client that could be unpredictably violent when residents fought. I sat next to the client. The client watched the two residents yell and argue as my colleague attempted to mediate. The client had an amused look on his face as if he were enjoying the conflict. He suddenly turned to me and said clearly and directly, "I watched the Christians get fed to lions in the Coliseum!" As he said it, he had a manic look on his face. That was the only time I saw him that way. At other times, he appeared confused and mumbled.

Casting Out Evil Spirits

Years later, the same colleague said that he met with a client who appeared to be possessed. During the session, he silently used his Priesthood to cast the evil spirit out. It was as if two things were going on at once; the visible session, which was calm and ordinary, and the invisible spiritual battle, which was intense.

I always dedicate my offices to be filled with the Holy Spirit and to be places of peace and healing. I've seen clients appear to feel relieved in my office, as if they were free of some temptation or torment for an hour a week. It's possibly one of the best gifts I could give them.

Spiritual Warfare

I treated and adolescent girl with suicidal thoughts. By the end of the session, her countenance had brightened considerably. That evening, I was awakened by what felt like an evil presence trying to harm me. This situation is what an evangelical Catholic friend of mine calls "spiritual warfare." I commanded the evil presence to leave in the name of Jesus Christ, and it went away. When things like this happen, my first thought is, "What did I do wrong?" I prayed to know what made it happen. I felt a spiritual impression that this evil spirit was angry with me because I had helped the adolescent girl earlier that day, and it wanted revenge.

Some clients do better while they are with me then get worse after they leave. It reminds me of Matthew 12:43-44, as follows:

> When the unclean spirit is gone out of a man, he walketh through dry places seeking rest, and findeth none. Then he saith, I will return into my house from whence I came out; and when he is come, he findeth it empty, swept, and garnished. Then goeth he, and taketh with himself seven other spirits more wicked than himself, and they enter in and dwell there: and the last state of that man is worse than the first.

My brother said on his mission, the Elders attempted to cast an evil spirit out of a member, but it resisted. The Elders told the member that he had moral agency and could choose to be free of the evil spirit. They were then able to successfully cast it out.

One of the scariest experiences I had was with a ten-year-old, Hispanic boy. His mother and adult sister brought him in because he was having "trances" and breaks with reality. As they sat in my office, he spoke in low, soothing tones, saying things to his mother like, "I don't have a mental illness. You have a mental illness. You're depressed. You're going to lose your mind. You're going to attempt suicide." I was surprised at how one so young could say such evil things to his own mother!

Hallucinations

As a Marriage and Family Therapist, I have treated clients with hallucinations. When a person has an audio hallucination, that person's brain shows the same neurological activity as if that person heard an actual voice. One theory of hallucination is that the brain connections are damaged in a way that when one portion of the brain imagines a voice, the other portion doesn't know it is imagined and perceives it as real.

Another theory of hallucinations is that there is an actual voice that is beyond the audio perception of most people, but that the affected person can hear.

Some spiritual experiences are easy to understand because they happen to more than one person. Two or more people can talk about the experience and help each other understand it.

Hallucinations are more difficult to understand because shared hallucinations are rare. I have had a client who experienced a shared hallucination, but he and his girlfriend were using drugs at the time and could have been open to suggestibility.

The majority of hallucinations are usually only experienced by one person at a time. I worked in a crisis residential setting in which many clients were having hallucinations simultaneously, but none picked up on the hallucinations of others, only their own. If hallucinations are from an outside source, why do they usually only target one person at a time?

Brain Damage

One theory of hallucinations is that they are caused by brain damage. Scientific studies show that Marijuana and Methamphetamine use can result in hallucinations. Substance use is especially dangerous while the brain is still developing. Children already have "magical thinking." Brain damage by substance use could stop their brains from developing beyond early stages.

Rain Man

When I was at BYU, I saw Kim Peek, the inspiration for Dustin Hoffman's character in Rain Man (1988). Kim stood on stage and multiplied numbers faster than we could with our calculators. He also calculated the day of the week for past and future dates. Unfortunately, he needed help to drive and find his way around the campus.

Kim's brain damage resulted in greatly enhanced brain functioning in some areas and greatly diminished brain functioning in others areas.

I studied photographic memories in college. I wished I had a photographic memory at test time! Some people who have it call it a curse because they remember everything, whether they want to or not, including trivial things.

Developing Psychoses

A client was struck by lightning while pregnant. It made her mouth, nose, eyes, and ears, and the top of her head bleed. She began hearing voices. Her son was born with birth marks like wings. Her head still hurts whenever the sky gets overcast.

A client with depression and substance use said that he and an atheist friend went to an abandoned town known as a gathering place for devil worshippers. The town ruins were covered with sigils. The man was curious. He took pictures of wisps of smoke coming from the ground. He saw a broken pentagram made out of rocks. He fixed it. Immediately, he felt a dark, heavy presence. He told his atheist friend. His atheist friend said he felt it too. They went home. The client felt more depressed than usual. His sight began dimming. He heard evil laughter. He took a shower and saw satanic symbols in the water. He looked at the pictures he had taken, but they were all smeared. He showed them to his mother, and she said she didn't see any smears. His father gave him a blessing. He felt better. His seeing and hearing problems went away.

Dissociation

Dissociation is a defense mechanism in which a person that cannot leave a situation physically leaves it mentally. A mild form of dissociation is daydreaming in class. A severe form of dissociation is a person fixating on a tangible point nearby while repressing everything else around. Some people dissociate to the point of having out of body experiences.

One of my clients was sexually abused. The next thing she knew, she was floating in a corner of the ceiling and looking down on her abuser and her body.

One of clients had been severely abused physically, sexually, emotionally, and religiously by her parents and her ex-husband. She was sitting in group therapy. A peer shared something that triggered my client's issues. She stood up to leave the room. The group leader told her to stay because they only had a few minutes left. She sat down. She looked out the door, which was ajar. The next moment, she was outside the door, looking back at her body in the chair.

Another time, she heard yelling outside her home. She peeked through a window and saw a woman hitting her front gate with a stick. She got scared and waited inside until the woman went away. She walked to the neighbor's house and asked if the neighbor had seen the woman hitting her front gate with a stick. The neighbor told her it was her. She said it wasn't. The neighbor said it was and pointed out my client's clothes. My client realized that she and the woman were wearing the same clothes. She went to the other neighbor and asked if she had been outside, hitting her front gate with a stick. The other neighbor confirmed that she had.

One of my clients discovered she had alternate personalities after writing in her journal. First, her writing appeared smooth with calm words. Then, her writing appeared pointy with cussing and anger. After that, her writing became smooth again. She didn't remember writing the angry part. She wondered if someone else had written it, or if she had written it with her other hand. She talked about it with her therapist who told her about alternate personalitities.

Some of my clients with alternate personalities are able to combine them together again. One of my colleagues counseled a woman with five personalities. The woman wasn't able to combine them. Instead, she carried a bag with five rocks, one for each personality. When she had to make important decisions, she would pull the rocks out and vote with them. Then, she followed what the majority chose.

Symbolism

I trained with Dr. Vincent Felitti who did the famous ACES study. One experience that led to the study was working with morbidly obese patients. He realized that obesity had to do with psychology more than physiology. For example, one woman was sexually abused as a child. As an adult, she got a job making sure elderly people in a nursing home stayed in their beds. It was symbolic of her wish to protect her younger self from her perpetrator sneaking out of his bed at night. The woman was able to lose over a hundred pounds. An elderly man at work made a sexual comment at her. She gained all the weight back.

I worked with a seventeen-year-old who had been sexually abused as a child. She wanted to become an anesthesiologist. It was symbolic of her wanting to numb the pain.

Alien Abduction

As a therapist, I am curious about the psychology of people's experiences. I tend to approach new experiences with an open mind. I have had many child clients testify in Court, but their testimonies were not believed. For that reason, I give my clients the benefit of the doubt until I know differently. I have also had clients who made false statements then later acknowledged having done so.

Early in my career, I read Edith Fiore's book, "Encounters: A Psychologist Reveals Case Studies of Abductions by Extra-Terrestrials" (1997: Ballentine Books, New York City). The trauma of the victims seemed real to me, but I was skeptical of alien abductions. Interestingly, the notes in the back said that many of the subjects had surgical procedures around the same times as their "abductions." My conclusion was that many of the subjects had difficulty with their anesthesia and became conscious or partially conscious during their surgeries, and interpreted their surgeries as abductions.

I also saw James L. Thompson's book, "Aliens & UFOs: Messengers or Deceivers," about people in the Middle Ages seeing fairies, and people in modern times seeing aliens. He said they were all demons masquerading as fairies or aliens.

Mind-Body-Spirit

Many therapists talk about a mind-body-spirit connection. If this connection is in balance, all three parts of a person will thrive. If this connection is hampered, all three parts will suffer.

I attended a training by Peter A. Levine, PhD, author of "Waking the Tiger: Healing Trauma" (1997). He talked about treating a woman who had been in the 9-11 terrorist attacks. She was working at her desk when there was an explosion, the lights went out, the whole building shook, and she was knocked onto the floor. She thought it was an earthquake. She heard a co-worker telling everyone to follow the co-worker's voice toward the stairs. She crawled toward the voice and touched a body.

When this woman came to see Dr. Levine, her body was stiff and rigid. She only moved normally from the neck up. She had dissociated from her body from the neck down. Through therapy, she was able to reconnect with her body as before the attack.

Many people dissociate from their bodies due to trauma. They view their bodies with loathing or with fear. This has a negative effect on their bodies, which grow unhealthy, weak, or fat. When these people reconnect with their bodies, they learn to manage, love, and nurture their bodies. They feel joy, and their bodies get healthier.

Satanic Ritual Abuse

Satanic Ritual Abuse (SRA) is a controversial topic. It caused a moral panic in the 1980s and 90s. Since then, society has minimized the effects Satanism while it grows more prevalent. Satanic images are becoming increasingly common, including devils, fire, "666," "13," and many symbols which are more subtle than these. A casual glance at celebrities, sports figures, and the media confirm this. Satanists are becoming increasingly visible while professing to have only positive effects on society. Isaiah prophesied about this, "Woe unto them that call evil good, and good evil; that put darkness for light, and light for darkness" (5:20)!

In my research, I found many articles about SRA, including a signed confession by Anne Davis' mother and stepfather (See Hell Minus One: My Story of Deliverance from Satanic Ritual Abuse and My Journey to Freedom, 2008: Transcript Bulletin Publishing, Tooele, Utah).

There are many reasons why SRA is difficult to prove: 1.) SRA perpetrators rely on secrecy, including masking their identities. 2.) They choose young victims who are less believable in court. 3.) They drug their victims to confuse their victims' memories. 4.) They control their victims through Stockholm Syndrome. 5.) They form alter personalities in their victims so their victims have difficulty remembering what happened.

When I worked in a group home for children and teens in Sioux Falls, South Dakota, one girl had a mental breakdown on Halloween. She said "they" were going to come after her. When my coworker told her she was on the second floor and was safe, she said they would climb onto the roof and take her out through the window. My coworker asked her who "they" were. She said her mother was the leader of a witch coven, and she had been groomed to take her mother's place when her mother died. She said she had witnessed babies being sacrificed.

My coworker made a report. The Federal Bureau of Investigation came out. They found the farms and barns that the girl described. They found lots of animal bones, but no human ones.

In Susanville, California, I met a victim of SRA at Church. He had a pentagram tattooed on the top of his right hand, which he kept covered. He also had various satanic tattoos on his body. He said that these were his marks to identify him to cult members. He said the punishment for leaving the cult was death, and he lived in constant fear. He said his grandfather was the head of the cult. He said when he was young, his grandfather and other cult members would meet in graveyards at night and gang-rape his sister and him. As a consequence, he was HIV positive.

Return to Innocence

Kirk Martin was the leader of a satanic heavy metal band. He loved nothing better than to shout obscenities into a crowd and hear them shout obscenities back. He worked for years to get a record contract. One night, he made a pact with Satan. Within a few days, he was offered the contract. Then, an elderly man sat in front of Kirk at a restaurant and told him that it wasn't his fault that he was sexually abused as a child. Kirk hadn't told anyone about the sexual abuse, including his parents and friends. The man left the diner and walked around the corner. Kirk followed him around the corner, but he was gone. He had only been out of Kirk's eyesight for seconds. That night, Kirk had a spiritual experience that included seeing a review of his life. He asked God to take him or change him. He gave his life to Jesus Christ. The next morning, he woke up and felt like a young child. He said, "The clouds were a little fluffier, the grass greener, the birds chirpier" (See https://blog.godreports.com/2012/09/the-heavy-metal-satanist-rescued-by-christ/). Jesus said, "Ye must be born again" (John 3:7). He also said, "Verily I say unto you, Except ye be converted, and become as little children, ye shall not enter into the kingdom of heaven" (Matthew 18:3).

Hollywood

Hollywood is the world's "holy wood" of worship of the devil.

In "Pop Music and Morality" (1982: Embryo Books, Salt Lake City, Utah), Lex de Azevedo writes about how musicians use music to persuade us to entertain thoughts that we never would otherwise, including thoughts of sex, suicide, and devil worship.

Movies and television are powerful ways to convey information. Though not evil by themselves, they can be used for evil purposes. Many people involved in Hollywood speak of "selling their souls to the devil," either figuratively or literally.

Some writers of books, poems, movies and music talk about automatic writing, or writing for another force, either spiritual or subconscious. Automatic writing has allegedly been used for entire movie scripts and song lyrics. Mae West told "Interview" magazine (1974: New York City) that spirits of men that "look nice" appear to her and give her stories for movie scripts. One of her biggest hits, "I'm No Angel" (1933), was reportedly written this way.

Mae West was described as single-handedly leading a sexual revolution. Before she was finished, the pendulum of popular opinion swung the other way.

Shirley Temple became the new leading movie star, presenting a more family-oriented theme.

Led Zeppelin reportedly used automatic writing for their songs. They followed Aleister Crowley, the so-called "Master Satanist of the 20th Century."

As an adolescent, I watched David Bowie's video for "Ashes to Ashes" (1980). It showed David dressed up like a clown, walking in front of a steamroller. I thought it was weird. As an adult, I interpreted it as a symbol of the futility of life followed closely by death, and it began to make more sense.

As an adolescent, I enjoyed David's movie, Labryinth (1986). As an adult, I had a more critical eye. The Goblin King, played by David, is obviously an allusion to the devil attempting to seduce the lead character to "sell her soul" to him by promising to be her slave. His song, "Underground" says, "It's only forever / Not long at all," as if in reference to hell. It also talks about rejection and says, "Don't tell me truth hurts, little girl / 'Cause it hurts like hell / But down in the underground / You'll find someone true / Down in the underground / A land serene, a crystal moon." This seems to show hell and the devil as a refuge for rejection and the pain of life. David famously promoted sexual alternatives. His videos to his last song are also filled with references to the death, hell, and the devil.

In one video interview, David lamented that his songs didn't sell better in the United States of America. He cites "puritanical values" as the reason for not doing so well. He says "puritanical values" as if they're bad. God bless puritanical values!

<u>Sympathy for the Devil</u>

Ever since the Rolling Stones sang "Sympathy for the Devil" (1968), modern Western culture has become more and more accepting of Satanism.

Elder Gene R. Cook was on a plane when Mick Jagger sat down next to him. Elder Cook asked Mick how rock and roll affects young people. Mick said as quoted by Elder Cook, "Our music is calculated to drive the kids to sex." Mick said he was just making money. Mick also knew some things about the Church of Jesus Christ of Latter-day Saints and told Elder Cook that he had had a few discussions with missionaries, but that he didn't believe in God or life after death. (Elder Gene R. Cook, 1989, "The Eternal Nature of the Law of Chastity," a talk at Rick's college.)

The "heartagram" is a mixture of a heart and a pentagram by Ville Valo, lead singer of the Finnish heavy metal band, HIM. Ville says his heartagram is not satanic. I am skeptical because of his many other references to the devil, including "666" and the unabbreviated name of his band, "His Infernal Majesty"!

The heartagram could be viewed as a symbol that the devil loves you. The devil would have you believe he loves you. His version of love is to accept you just the way you are, and to give you whatever you want—until he has all power over you. He wants to torture you forever.

The rise of the Baphomet Statue opposite the Ten Commandments at the Oklahoma City Court House is a symbol for the crossroads we face in our nation and world. Do we choose the devil, or do we choose God? One path leads to physical and spiritual death; the other to resurrection and eternal life.

Modern Ritualistic Behavior

John Wycliffe was a Christian reformer who preached the gospel of Jesus Christ in purity and plainness. James Resby, one of his followers, refused to renounce Wycliffe's teachings. Resby was the first Christian Reformer executed in Scotland in 1405. That same year, the University of St. Andrews was established. This pattern appears to be repeated across the Western world, though not in such synchronicity. The plain gospel of Jesus Christ was rejected. Institutions of so-called "higher learning" were founded to teach supposedly complicated religious knowledge. These institutions eventually became secular.

The University of St. Andrews was also the site of the burning of Protestant reformers, including Patrick Hamilton. To this day, students avoid stepping on the cobblestone marked "PH" for fear it will cause them to do badly in their studies. If they do, they can atone by running around the university backwards and naked eight times. Doing anything backwards is a sign of Satanism, according to Aleister Crowley. Running around naked reminds one of ancient Celtic Druidic paganism. Another way to atone is by staying up all night and swimming in the North Sea at dawn on Mayday. Mayday is a pagan holiday. This is not to accuse students of pagan and satanic practices, but to point out the strange, but non-coincidental roots of modern ritualistic behavior.

Another example of this is the "Festival of Colors" in various places in the Western World, including Utah. It's basically a big party in which people throw colored powder or water on each other. How else do you get young Christians to attend a Hindu worship ritual?

Isaiah describes how we will view Lucifer, "They that shall see thee shall narrowly look upon thee, and consider thee, saying is this the man that mad the earth to tremble, that did shake kingdoms; that made the world as a wilderness, and destroyed the cities thereof; that opened not the house of his prisoners?" In other words, we will be amazed at how one bodiless spirit could corrupt a whole world of people with bodies, including ourselves!

Dual Identity

I went to training by Dr. Ira Chasnoff, an expert in Addiction. She said that all addiction involves a dual identity.

One of my clients was a thirteen-year-old who sexually abused his younger sister. His parents sent him to live with his grandmother. She began parenting him with discipline, teaching him to act responsibly, and he did, but he though she was too strict. While he was seeing me, he went to an art therapist who had him mold and paint a mask. The next time I saw him, he was excited. He told me all about his "goblin" mask. It was green with slanted eyes and a large smile. Shortly afterwards, his grandmother sent him to live in foster care. He had become completely unruly. Did the mask bring out his true identity? Did it free his mind from his perceived restrictions of responsible behavior?

Mind Control

Mind Control is an ancient science. It is also practiced in modern times, including by the Nazis and satanic cults.

The Nazis forced soldiers to raise dogs then kill them. This is a common form of mind control because when you bond with an animal, killing it means killing part of your conscience.

I read about an anonymous person's experience growing up in a satanic cult. He said he was brainwashed as a child to believe he was not human. He said his handlers, the people who perpetrated the mind control, would introduce him to pets, allow him to bond with them, then kill them.

Truddi Chase wrote about her experiences being mind controlled in "When Rabbit Howls" (1990: Penguin Publishing Group, London). Her experiences at a young age resulted in over ninety alter egos.

The United States government conducted unethical mind control studies in the 1950s, 60s, and 70s. They used various mind control drugs. They did not get permission from their subjects. They targeted drug dealers and prostitutes. They also targeted college students, including Ted Kaczynski, who had permanent brain damage and later became known as the Unabomber.

Dave Grossman, in his book, "On Killing" (1995: Little, Brown and Company, Boston, Massachusetts) describes various mind control techniques that the military uses to turn empathetic human beings into trained killers. Handlers of some special forces use mind control to protect their soldiers. They train their soldiers to form alter egos that carry out utilitarian missions. If the soldiers are captured and tortured for information, the soldiers say they don't know and appear believable because that knowledge is part of their alter egos. This kind of training can also be used to exploit soldiers. Sometimes, they are commanded to commit atrocities under the guise of their alter egos. This form of mind control doesn't last forever. When people return home and begin to feel safe and stable for a long period of time, their alter egos naturally begin to re-connect with their original selves, causing stress and confusion. The movie, Jacob's Ladder (1990), somewhat portrays this process.

The movie, The Bourne Identity (2002), portrays Jason Bourne, a sleeper assassin who has been mind-controlled to kill a foreign leader. Jason, who doesn't even know his real identity, overcomes his mind control programming and begins to make decisions for himself. His handlers consider him a "rogue agent" and send other sleeper assassins to kill him.

Positive Mind Control?

The self-help movement promotes mind control for your own benefit. This includes hypnosis, self-hypnosis, affirmations, mantras, meditation, and more. Some of these are negative.

When I was a missionary in Florida, my companions and I would see women in immodest clothes and joke, "Sing a hymn, Elder, sing a hymn!"

Singing hymns is a form of self-control of the mind. So is saying a prayer. So is reciting a scripture in your mind or out loud.

Joyce Meyers wrote "Battlefield of the Mind" (2002: Warner Faith, New York City) about how the devil tries to manipulate our thinking, getting us to believe in false, negative ideas.

To combat the temptations of the devil, we need to control our thoughts. We do this by praying and reading scriptures every day. Non-religious people might view this as a form of mind control. If it is, it is the best kind. It teaches us to control our thoughts and to think like our Father in Heaven.

Raised from the Dead

I have had many clients who have died and have

been resuscitated. One woman was a victim of domestic violence. One man had died six times from drug overdose.

There are many videos on youtube of people being raised from the dead. Some have been dead for three days or more. According to Science, they should be brain-dead after four minutes with no Oxygen. These are things scientists and doctors can't explain.

Resurrection

Matthew 27:52 says, "And the graves were opened; and many bodies of the saints which slept arose." We members of the Church of Jesus Christ of Latter-day Saints believe that all people will be resurrected and that their bodies will be perfect. It is a glorious doctrine. Non-Christians may view it with caution or fear.

Zombies

The devil twists the truth. Are zombies the devil's version of the resurrection of the dead?

The mother of one of my clients told me that her son and his friends speak about "the Zombie Apocalypse" like it's a real thing. Even if they don't believe in it literally, maybe they do metaphorically. It seems to be in the Zeitgeist.

Revelations

Revelations talks about the end of the world. It's not a pretty sight. Even as I write this, worries about the Coronavirus spreading are causing business, travel, and social shut downs. I hope the Coronavirus is just practice for what is described in Revelations. It makes sense to me that God will not cause overwhelming cataclysms until He has given us plenty of warning in smaller catastrophes beforehand.

Conclusion

We are not human beings having a spiritual experience.
We are spiritual beings having a human experience—
Pierre Teilhard de Chardin

Our mainstream Western culture discourages spiritual expression, including Christians sharing their beliefs with non-Christians. Eastern and indigenous cultures encourage spirituality.

Many people do not talk about their spiritual experiences with others. Some find their experiences too sacred to share. Some do not want to share too much about the negative aspect of spirituality. Some do not want to be viewed as weird or even insane by others.

Mental illness and spirituality are different, but they do relate to each other. Some people feel more comfortable sharing their spiritual experiences in therapy.

Spirituality can be positive or negative just as life can be.

It is natural to have curiosity about spiritual phenomena. To deny the existence of spiritual phenomena is to deny a part of ourselves, our own beings. We do so at our own peril. Conversely, to embrace spirituality is to understand who we truly are and what our supreme destiny can be.